Improving
Student Learning
One Principal
at a Time

ASCD MEMBER BOOK

Many ASCD members received this book as a
member benefit upon its initial release.

Learn more at: **www.ascd.org/memberbooks**

ASCD cares about Planet Earth.
This book has been printed on environmentally friendly paper.

JANE E. POLLOCK
SHARON M. FORD

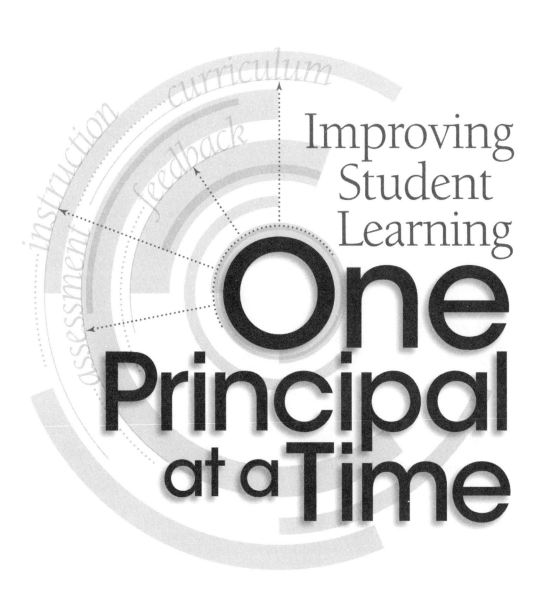

Improving
Student
Learning
One
Principal
at a Time

Association for Supervision and Curriculum Development ■ Alexandria, Virginia USA

Association for Supervision and Curriculum Development
1703 N. Beauregard St. • Alexandria, VA 22311-1714 USA
Phone: 800-933-2723 or 703-578-9600 • Fax: 703-575-5400
Web site: www.ascd.org • E-mail: member@ascd.org
Author guidelines: www.ascd.org/write

Gene R. Carter, *Executive Director;* Nancy Modrak, *Publisher;* Julie Houtz, *Director of Book Editing & Production;* Katie Martin, *Project Manager;* Georgia Park, *Senior Graphic Designer;* Mike Kalyan, *Production Manager;* Cynthia Stock, *Typesetter;* Sarah Plumb, *Production Specialist*

All Web links in this book are correct as of the publication date below but may have become inactive or otherwise modified since that time. If you notice a deactivated or changed link, please e-mail books@ascd.org with the words "Link Update" in the subject line. In your message, please specify the Web link, the book title, and the page number on which the link appears.

ASCD Member Book, No. FY09-5 (February 2009, P). ASCD Member Books mail to Premium (P) and Select (S) members on this schedule: Jan., PS; Feb., P; Apr., PS; May, P; July, PS; Aug., P; Sept., PS; Nov., PS; Dec., P. Select membership was formerly known as Comprehensive membership.

PAPERBACK ISBN: 978-1-4166-0768-7   ASCD product #109006
Also available as an e-book through ebrary, netLibrary, and many online booksellers (see Books in Print for the ISBNs).

Quantity discounts for the paperback edition only: 10–49 copies, 10%; 50+ copies, 15%; for 1,000 or more copies, call 800-933-2723, ext. 5634, or 703-575-5634. For desk copies: member@ascd.org.

Library of Congress Cataloging-in-Publication Data

Pollock, Jane E., 1958–
   Improving student learning one principal at a time / Jane E. Pollock, Sharon M. Ford.
      p.   cm.
   Includes bibliographical references and index.
   ISBN 978-1-4166-0768-7 (pbk. : alk. paper) 1. School principals—United States. 2. Teacher-principal relationships—United States. 3. Academic achievement—United States. 4. Educational leadership—United States. I. Ford, Sharon M. II. Title.

   LB2831.62.P65 2009
   371.2'012—dc22

                                    2008042690

18 17 16 15 14 13 12 11 10 09   1 2 3 4 5 6 7 8 9 10 11 12

To our friend, Ilene Block.

*To my sisters and brothers who played school
with me in Venezuela: Beth, Jimmy, and Johnny;
Sandy, the associate head of school;
and Bobby, the principal.*

–JEP

*With appreciation to my husband, Gary, for his ongoing
encouragement; my sister, Carol, for her wise words;
my mother, Doris, for her loving support; my father,
Don, for encouraging my work in education;
and my cousin, Charles W. De Pue,
former superintendent of schools.*

–SMF

Improving Student Learning
One Principal at a Time

Introduction

Horace knows that the status quo is the problem. Only by examining the existing compromises . . . and moving beyond them to better compromises, can one form a more thoughtful school. And only in thoughtful schools can thoughtful students be hatched.

Theodore R. Sizer, *Horace's School*

LAYNE PARMENTER, PRINCIPAL OF URIE ELEMENTARY SCHOOL IN LYMAN, WYOMING, sent Jane E. Pollock, one of this book's authors, an e-mail that read as follows:

> Thanks for working with our teachers last week on lesson planning and research-based instructional strategies. They liked the lesson planning schema—the way of organizing instruction by deliberately targeting how to strengthen feedback to students in order to markedly improve their performances on district curriculum standards.

> Say, I was thinking that maybe you have some ideas about conferencing with teachers before and after I observe their classes. I use the district evaluation forms and procedures, of course, but speaking honestly, these forms and procedures don't really help me, as a school supervisor, discuss how a teacher should teach better so that students will learn better. I've been so busy with all of my other administrative "duties as assigned" that I have not developed a good way to communicate instructional suggestions specifically about *learning* and not just about the teaching.

A few days later, Jane received another e-mail, this time from Mike, a high school teacher:

> Picture this: I'm a little nervous about going to my post-observation conference. I have the recognizable structure to my lesson. I also have a great, positive tone in my classroom, and students are engaged in the learning. But there's something horribly wrong:. I look through my grade book and see about seven students in each class failing, with Ds and Fs. That's about 30 students in the four 9th grade English classes I teach . . . more than a quarter of my students. What is my appraising administrator going to say about those data?

> Much to my surprise, nothing. During my post-observation conference, there is no mention of the failures in my classes. I get glowing remarks about my lesson, the positive-feeling tone, and the fact that all students appeared to be engaged. I should be happy about this, but I leave the conference with mixed emotions because I *know* something's wrong with my teaching. How could I get such a glowing appraisal when more than 25 percent of my students are doing so poorly? Maybe I don't understand—are evaluation and supervision supposed to be the same process?

> Reflecting on my teaching, I planned lessons using the district curriculum guide and approved textbook, and I designed great activities organized to fit the time frame (even with good transitions), but I wasn't conscientiously assessing what students knew. I had the superficial pieces of teaching in place, but I was missing that significant element of feedback that you say would help my students perform better.

> Who is supposed to help me improve student learning if my supervisor doesn't address this during an appraisal?

After receiving these e-mails, Jane contacted Sharon M. Ford, who had recently retired as assistant professor at the University of Colorado at Denver, where she taught graduate supervision courses in the Administrative Leadership and Policy Studies program. Both Layne (the principal) and Mike (the teacher) recognized that classroom observations had merit for teacher-evaluation purposes, but both sensed the need for a different approach to observations for supervision purposes: a way to help a principal and a teacher collaborate to improve student performance. Accordingly, Jane asked Sharon if she had any research on evaluating and supervising teaching to improve student learning that would be pertinent to both a principal and a teacher.

As we, Sharon and Jane, perused the literature together, we discussed the ways in which various models of evaluation and supervision fostered more effective schooling and concluded that the ones that were most supportive of this goal repeatedly targeted teacher actions, professional development, and improvements in the collegial relationship between administrator and teacher. However, we noted that although improving student achievement is a frequently stated goal of supervision, there are actually very few supervision strategies explicitly aimed at this target. Yes, the supervisory role focuses on improving both teaching and learning, but many actual methods of supervision focus heavily on *teacher* behaviors and attitudes, assuming that *learner* gains will happen as a result of teachers reflecting upon and possibly changing their practices. As Mike's e-mail indicates, this does not necessarily follow.

Our investigation continued. We revisited the history of supervision, looking at the evolution of its role and purpose in education. We explored various approaches that supervisors have used to evaluate or coach teachers. We also interviewed school administrators and heard principals and teachers sounding a recurring theme: both considered supervision and evaluation tasks an add-on to their jobs—and one that seldom led to tangible improvements.

Have the demands on principals and teachers changed so much over time that supervision is no longer an effective means of improving teaching to improve learning? Do most teachers really approach their classroom observation as a "dog and pony show" aimed at pacifying supervisors? Do they expect the feedback they get from this observation to be inadequate and inconsequential? Has supervision become unfeasible for principals who, by their own admission, follow evaluation protocol to judge teaching and professionalism but are uncertain about how to give teachers useful and effective feedback that will help students learn better?

We examined more than 100 years of nationwide population changes, both for students and for the teaching force; business management practices adopted by schools; the impact of events such as wars and the Sputnik satellite program; the introduction of collective bargaining; and the increasing diversity of students. These factors all contributed to the ways supervision shifted from inspection models, to leadership frameworks, to clinical supervision models, to models advocating for social justice, to today's standards movement fueled by accountability fever. Our conversations were alternatively complicated, when considering past events and factors that influenced supervision, and lucid, when reflecting on the patterns that surfaced in supervision trends in education.

The Focus and Purpose of Supervision

Throughout the history of education, supervision's focus has always been the teacher, and its stated goal has been the improvement of instructional practices. The complication is that supervision originally served two purposes: eliminating ineffective teachers who were deficient in skills and strengthening the overall school organization. For this reason, administrators have had to simultaneously perform roles of evaluator and supervisor and balance the seemingly contradictory goals of "evaluating" and "improving." This has often placed administrators and teachers in a "we/they" position, diminishing their opportunities to work together for improvement of learning.

As Sergiovanni and Starratt (1993) point out, supervision has become increasingly cooperative and focused on the clear goal of instructional improvement. The way that the process has gradually expanded to include the teacher in the discussion about what the supervisor observes is evidence of this evolution. However, only recently have the teacher's students—their progress and achievement—become a focus for supervisors. But looking at student work and progress as a factor of a teacher's instructional effectiveness is still not a widespread supervision practice; when it is done, the data considered are almost exclusively summative achievement data, and the primary question considered is whether overall student achievement improves from one year to the next, rather than what ongoing effects individual teachers have on individual student performance as the school year progresses.

Changing Supervision

When comparing the traditional, managerial evaluation practices that sought to remove weak employees with more recent forms of supportive supervision that cultivate a relationship between supervisor and teacher, it is clear that the goals of supervision have not specified formative tasks to explicitly improve student learning. Current research on learning, however, suggests that we can successfully develop a new approach to supervising teachers that results in improved learning for all students.

We know that the quality of a teacher's planning, delivery, and assessment significantly affects student learning (Tucker & Stronge, 2005) and that student success increases when teachers use certain instructional strategies (see Marzano, Pickering, & Pollock, 2001). Teachers can deliberately change their practices to achieve gains for their students, as evidenced by external test scores, and they can also boost all learners' knowledge retention and application rates, as evidenced by classroom data and reports. A supervisory tool, used by teachers and principals in collaboration, can provide the technical assistance teachers need to make those sound instructional decisions. Such a tool can also strengthen the principal's ability to examine student results with a teacher, who can, in turn, take immediate action aimed at improving instruction and learning for that cohort of students. A good supervisory tool generates timely feedback on student performance—and thus, teacher performance—that teachers can act on immediately. Contrast this with the months of time that pass before student results in the form of external measures or state tests can be brought to a staff's attention.

In this book, we turn our attention to the powerful role that every principal can play in improving supervisor–teacher communication, instructional efficiency, and, ultimately, student learning. What we present here is an extension of the research and ideas explored in Jane's book *Improving Student Learning One Teacher at a Time* (Pollock, 2007), in which she wrote that an individual teacher furthers student advancement by adhering to the fundamentals she calls the "Big Four":

1. *Use a well-articulated curriculum.* Institute clearly articulated, "just-right" grade-level curriculum standards (benchmarks).

2. *Plan for delivery.* Plan and deliver instruction using the Teaching Schema for Master Learners with research-based instructional strategies.

3. *Vary assessment.* Assessment methods should cover a wide range of formal and informal methods and should include frequent formative as well as summative assessment.

4. *Give criterion-based feedback.* Revitalize feedback methods, including scoring to grade-level curriculum standards (benchmarks) in grade books and generating reports that more accurately inform students, parents or guardians, and team members about student progress.

Teachers who apply the recommended techniques for each of these four areas generate better student performances and improve their communication with students and their parents and guardians. Although these areas seem like obvious targets for schools undergoing reform, most school-improvement initiatives focus on only one at a time; it is employing all of the Big Four in tandem that is critical for making gains.

In her book, Jane also encouraged teachers to use the Teaching Schema for Master Learners (see Step 2 in the Big Four) to plan their daily teaching, because the Schema provides a way to introduce all elements of the Big Four—a just-right curriculum; well-structured, research-based instruction; varied assessment; and targeted feedback—into every lesson.

The steps in the Schema (and step abbreviations that form the acronym "GANAG") are as follows*:

1. Set the learning goal— curriculum standard and benchmarks (G)
   Opportunity for feedback
2. Access prior student knowledge (A)
   Opportunity for feedback
3. Acquire new information—declarative or procedural (N)
   Opportunity for feedback
4. Apply thinking skills or use knowledge in new situations (A)
   Opportunity for feedback
5. Generalize or summarize learning back to learning goal (G)
   Opportunity for feedback
6. Assign homework, if necessary

---

*The discussion of the Teaching Schema for Master Learners in Jane's book *Improving Student Learning One Teacher at a Time* (2007) featured a different abbreviation scheme: GO for *set the learning goal/benchmarks*, APK for *access prior knowledge*, NI for *acquire new information,* APP for *apply thinking skills or real-world situation,* and GEN for *generalize/summarize.* The current shorthand, abbreviating to GANAG, reflects the way practitioners have come to talk about the Schema.

The Schema acts as a scaffold for connecting the curriculum directly to instruction and assessment by illuminating the importance of giving feedback to help ensure student progress on the grade-level curriculum standards. Every lesson is, in a sense, a microcosm of the Big Four.

In this book, we present an adaptation of the Teaching Schema for Master Learners (and, by extension, the Big Four) for principals and others who perform supervisory duties within a school. The consensus that supervisors' classroom observations can invigorate teaching and learning confirms our decision to focus improvement efforts on the procedures supervisors use during the observation and the post-observation conference. We believe the center of attention for the supervisor–teacher discussion must be what the learner is learning as a result of the teacher's instruction and ongoing feedback. This shared goal guides professional dialogue prior to the classroom observation, serves as an advance organizer for the supervisor as he or she transcribes the events of a lesson, and guides analysis after the classroom observation.

The first chapter in this book provides a historical overview of the adjustments that have been made to supervision over the years and how those adjustments affected teaching and learning. Each subsequent chapter discusses specific techniques that principals and other supervisors can apply to the beginning, middle, and end of a classroom observation. Finally, we discuss the critical role a principal can play using the data gleaned from teachers' grade books, from grades on report cards, and from common local assessments and state or national test results.

Between the chapters, we hear from supervisors who report on the reality of the work we propose. These administrators describe their experiences adapting the steps of the Teaching Schema for Master Learners to their existing practices and how, in doing so, they have helped to improve student learning—one principal at a time.

1

From Inspection to Improvement

After reading this chapter, you should be able to

• Explain how the focus of supervision evolved from improving the institution and its employees to improving students' learning.
• Describe the challenges and turning points in the profession of educational supervision.

ROB BECKER, AN EXPERIENCED PRINCIPAL, SHARED POSITIVE INSIGHTS WITH US ABOUT supervising and evaluating teachers in a building where 70 percent of students qualify for free and reduced-price lunch. Rob confirmed that the district evaluation policy clearly addresses needs of veteran and probationary teachers and was developed with the intent of helping principals like him complete formative and summative evaluations to improve teaching. However, when we asked Rob about the ways in which his district's guidelines for supervision and evaluation specifically target improving student learning, he paused before giving this thoughtful and revealing reply:

> It seems that they *should*, but I think that particular message of supervision and evaluation has been implicit, whereas the goal to improve teaching and professionalism has been explicit. It would be really easy to wrap my practices deliberately around improving student learning. Why hasn't that been identified more succinctly in the research and literature? Honestly, it just makes sense.

Does Improving Teaching Always Improve Learning?

The more principals we interviewed, the more interested we became in answering this question: Why is it that the goals of supervision are to improve both teaching and student performance, yet traditional supervision strategies focus primarily on the teacher's teaching, generally minimizing or even ignoring growth in student learning? Moreover, why are some supervisory visits to classrooms viewed as supportive while others are dreaded and seen as occasional events of perfunctory judgment? Why do principals feel as though they must act as both collaborative instructional leaders and critical evaluative administrators—roles that many find difficult if not impossible to reconcile?

Although a vast literature base indicates that educational supervision in the 21st century aims to improve learning for all students, the procedures principals follow continue to require them to concurrently evaluate teacher performance and coach teachers to reflect on and improve their instruction and assessment methods. We believe that we are at the promising point in history where we as educators *can* define a supervisory movement to improve student learning. The key is to implement the research findings on ways that teaching can positively affect learning.

What we should *not* do is continue to chase deadlines for "making teachers accountable" through communicating test scores and probable sanctions. If the education profession continues to focus on inspecting *summative student data*—and primarily using these data to determine which schools should be closed and which principals are "weak" and should be replaced—we will miss out on the myriad, research-supported ways that *classroom data* can inform better instructional and supervisory decisions. History convinces us that to take the road less traveled this time around offers the real reward we seek, which is improved student learning.

In this chapter, we take the time to describe the important evolution of our profession because it shows that while supervision had been adjusted on a continual basis to improve professionalism, there have been relatively few changes in practices designed to ensure gains in student achievement. As we continue to meet with supervisors, we find that retracing the historical milestones in the development of the profession (see Figure 1.1) not only helps supervisors

---

FIGURE 1.1

The Evolution of Educational Supervision

Pre-1900: Supervision as Inspection
Local citizens inspect facilities and instruction
Supervision based on intuition rather than technical knowledge

Early 1900: Scientific Organizational Improvement
Superintendents manage routines and inspect teachers
Frederick Taylor's *Principles of Scientific Management* (1916)
Time and motion tasks
Rating scales

1900–Midcentury: Teacher Improvement and the Democratic Motive
Move to abolish a narrow curriculum (Dewey)
Teaching "tasks" not like business "tasks" (Elliott)

1930s–1950s: Change and Collaboration
Supervisors as specialists
Expanding job market drives teaching adjustments

1960s–1970s: Clinical Supervision
Fostering leadership
Focus on improving rather than evaluating teaching

1980s: Teaching Behavior and Student Response
Effective teaching is teachable
Professional growth plans

1990s: Focus on the Learner
America 2000 and Goals 2000
Learning standards for students

2000s: Supervision for Improved Learning
Accountability
Standards-based improvement for learning and teaching

appreciate the foundations of their role but also clarifies the opportunity that now lies before us: to engineer contemporary educational goals rather than simply react to events.

The Earliest Model: Supervision as Inspection (Pre-1900)

The people who built colonial schools in North America and sent their children there varied in their customs by region, thus providing an interesting economic and geographic contrast between the New England, Mid-Atlantic, and Southern schools. The schools themselves ranged from the rural, one-room schoolhouses to town schools governed by selectmen to aptly named *moving schools* (led by traveling teachers). There were also *dame schools* run by women in their homes, private schools, and schools for trade apprenticeships. Teachers were generally orthodox schoolmasters preparing for work in the legal profession or young women seeking income. The most common curriculum included reading, writing, arithmetic, and often the religious catechism directed toward outwitting Satan, as exemplified by the Act of 1647 (Ornstein & Levine, 1993, p. 155). School supervisors during this era were respected local citizens whose function was to inspect schools to maintain strict standards for facilities and instruction.

This tradition of supervision by local inspection continued from the colonial period to the early 1800s, at which time various local government tax revenues financed the formation of school districts, and sometimes students paid a *rate bill* or tuition (Ornstein & Levine, 1993). Although elected officials managed the construction and maintenance of schools and raised tax revenue for their support, they acknowledged the need for district superintendents to take on the role of supervision of curriculum and instructional standards; the superintendents were considered to have more educational experience than local citizens. Teachers were hired by the elected school board, and certification "was a simple but chaotic process" (p. 171), because each community issued its own certificates and did not recognize the certificates of other districts.

By the 1840s, Horace Mann, a strong proponent of the common schools, recommended schooling for all children as a way to prepare the public for democracy, national identity, and purpose. Mann argued for teaching ethical, nonsectarian principles in schools and proposed providing public education to diverse populations that included large numbers of immigrants (Cremin, 1957). This helped increase school enrollment, particularly in the urban areas, and "school reform" became synonymous with establishing new strategies for organizational administration. The population shift also spawned the need for more teachers, thus establishing the *normal school* for teacher preparation (Gutek, 1991). For the field of supervision, this meant a new focus: adjusting managerial routines in the growing organization became the primary job of the administrator.

The 19th century ended with more dramatic economic and population changes predicated by the spread of industrialism and the end of the Civil War. As many one-room schoolhouses evolved into separate schools with grade levels, teachers had to change their instructional methods. Pressed to maintain high standards, supervisors adopted a new approach similar to the successful authoritarian approach used in industry. The superintendent, as the official head of the organization, was responsible for maintaining its efficiency; this meant inspecting teachers and their instructional practices.

The purpose of supervision during this era was to ensure efficiency by monitoring and overseeing curriculum and instruction and evaluating teacher performance and student achievement. Supervisors functioned primarily to instruct poorly prepared teachers to conform to standard practices. Inspection, often derided as "snoopervision," was the prevailing approach (Oliva, 1989, p. 5). According to Sullivan and Glanz (2005), literature of the period indicates that supervisors employed intuition, not technical knowledge, to assess teaching competency. Employees who were deemed inefficient and who seemingly could not be retrained were dismissed. The general tenor of the supervisor's role is well captured by a Massachusetts superintendent named Balliet, quoted in an 1894 *National Educational Association Proceedings* publication titled "What Can Be Done to Increase the Efficiency of Teachers in Actual Services?" Balliet stated that in order for a school to remain effective, it must "first, secure a competent superintendent; second, let him 'reform' all the teachers who are incompetent and can be 'reformed'; and third, bury the dead" (Sullivan & Glanz, 2005, p. 8). In this context and atmosphere, the supervisor gained high community status and respectability for his authority, even as teachers grew resentful of the supervisor's intrusiveness.

At this time, when the school size increased, a new layer of administration developed. *Special supervisors* were middle-level management, primarily women.

They had no formal training in supervision and were assigned to assist less experienced teachers through subject-area coaching in penmanship, art, and spelling. A second group of supervisors, primarily men, received the title of *general supervisors*. They too lacked formal training and provided subject-area assistance in mathematics, science, and management duties. Sullivan and Glanz (2005) observe that the general supervisors often usurped the special supervisors' roles and evolved to become assistant managers. "General supervisors," they note, "gained wider acceptance simply because they were men" (p. 13). Supervision was taking a turn toward coaching, but this new direction was derailed by a cultural sense that running an organization was properly the business of men.

By 1900, school supervisors had become organizational managers whose job requirements did include evaluating teacher performance and monitoring student achievement. However, while supervision accomplished much in the area of improving the organization, little improvement in teaching and learning seemed to have been attributed to the role or leadership of supervisors.

Scientific Organizational Improvement: Supervision in the Early 1900s

By 1900, school supervisors were firmly entrenched as organizational managers responsible for evaluating teacher performance and monitoring student achievement. In 1916, Frederick Taylor published *The Principles of Scientific Management*, in which he introduced *scientific management* as a way to conduct "a complete mental revolution on the part of people working under it" (Boone & Bowen, 1980, p. 35). Briefly, scientific management required careful selection of workers and subsequent development to support task accomplishment, collection of time- and task-data, worker incentives, and redivision of work to accommodate collaboration. According to Taylor, in the scientific management model, "the scientific selection of the workman and his progressive development represents a democracy, cooperation, a general division of work that will be profitable" (Boone & Bowen, 1980, p. 46).

In 1913, Franklin Bobbitt at the University of Chicago published an article titled "Some General Principles of Management Applied to the Problems of City-School Systems," in which he supported the application of scientific and control-oriented principles of supervision to schools. In 1924, James Hosic, a professor of education at Teachers College, Columbia University, spoke out strongly against Bobbitt's support for scientific management, arguing that "teaching cannot be 'directed' the same way as bricklaying" (Sullivan & Glanz, 2005, p. 14). Hosic advocated that supervisors move away from any remaining autocratic tendencies and toward more collaborative approaches with teachers. Nevertheless, the popularity of applying scientific approaches to supervision led to the task of gathering data using rating scales to retain strong teachers and eliminate weak ones. Schools were viewed as factories that shaped and turned out products (educated persons), and teachers undoubtedly were viewed as the laborers assigned to the task.

To incorporate the findings of scientific management into education, supervisors used rating scales as an allegedly objective means for promoting the efficiency of the school operation. While the responsibility of supervision continued to be applied as a service to eliminate weak employees, it now did so for the purpose of scientifically improving schools as organizations. However, there were no uniform standards for teacher efficiency or agreed-upon criteria for excellent teaching, and reliability in the use of rating scales was very low. Not surprisingly, teachers and other educators widely criticized the use of rating scales. During the subsequent 20 years, publications from the National Education Association denounced the practice and attempted to remove inspection by rating from supervision.

A final footnote about the evolution of supervision during this era included one residual but critical feature of industrialization. Specialized occupations had become accepted as a way to generate improvements in any field, and this movement accentuated a need for supervisors to be recognized as specialized professionals. The quandary supervisors faced was that their training had been geared toward applying inspection and rating techniques (largely to support salary decisions, promotions, and dismissals) rather than toward how to work cooperatively with teachers to improve instruction (Glanz, 1991). In other words, the model for the specialized field of supervision was set in response to research in factory production efficiency rather than created as a catalyst for improving teaching and learning. The role of the principal was to be an authoritarian inspector specializing in skills necessary to reform or dismiss an employee rather than to be an expert in pedagogy, willing and able to provide useful and meaningful feedback to teachers to improve student performance.

Teacher Improvement and the Democratic Motive: Supervision from 1900 through Mid-Century

While social optimism prevailed in the early 1900s and industrialization led to scientific management, educational progressivism gained attention. John Dewey combined ideas about democracy with an educational science by recommending an experiential, "learning by doing" methodology and a course of study requiring students to apply skills and knowledge for social usefulness. Curriculum showed more tolerance for students' interests, shifting from centralized and prescribed to more child centered. These changes naturally initiated changes in teaching. The use of memorization techniques as the primary means for learning and, via testing, as a determining factor in measuring student achievement began to give way to a focus on problem solving. And educators began to talk about the need to adapt supervision to these new models.

In our opinion, a significant milestone in supervision history occurred in 1914, when Edward C. Elliott, a science teacher and superintendent of schools in Leadville, Colorado, recognized supervision's unique capacity for improving teaching methods. Elliott noted that the "tasks" of teaching students were not as clearly "accomplished" as in business, and he redefined supervision as "the democratic motive of American education" (as cited in Pajak, 1993, p. 2). Elliott advocated separating administrative tasks for efficiency and supervisory tasks for instilling creativity.

Supervisors during this time began to take on more curriculum work as proof of their instructional expertise and their willingness to collaborate with teachers. However, their new teacher support role was hampered by a new tendency toward standardization. In the increasingly affluent country, supervisors were required to ensure homogeneity yet differentiate for learners by applying curriculum prescribed by the superintendent and the community—a curriculum introduced first by The Committee of Ten in 1892 and strengthened by the Cardinal Principles of Secondary Education in 1918 (Ornstein & Levine, 1993). Supervisors' efforts to support teachers were further hampered by the fact that educational success was commonly measured in rates of student attendance and completion— both of which had more to do with larger, societal factors than anything a school, supervisor, or teacher was or was not doing. So it was that "control" through alignment with administrative authoritarianism was the predominant descriptor of supervisors' work during the first two decades of the 20th century. However, Elliott's call for leadership through democracy would reemerge in latter decades to powerful effect.

There was another significant redefinition of supervision between the 1930s and the 1950s due largely to the dissonance created by the requirements for inspection and a new need for collaboration. Just as school organizations struggled to gain the reputation of being "efficient" in the eyes of the public, supervisors struggled to be recognized as valuable instructional leaders in the eyes of teachers. As the middle part of the 20th century brought increased urbanization and a wider range of employment opportunities, schools began focusing on educating students to take their place in the expanding job market. This stimulated a new mission for teachers and brought about a significant redefinition of supervision for principals. In 1931, A. S. Barr wrote that supervisors "must possess training in both the science of instructing pupils and the science of instructing teachers. Both are included in the science of supervision" (Sullivan & Glanz, 2005, p. 17).

Led by Romiett Stevens at Teachers College, Columbia University, teacher rating scales began to change to focus on improving instruction. Stevens supported the use of stenographic reports—verbatim accounts of classroom activities—as a more humanistic way to observe lessons and evaluate teacher efficiency than the previous practice of inspecting by "intuition." As these and other more democratic and professional supervisory procedures began to emerge, supervisors needed additional training in order to focus their work on improving instruction rather than just promoting and retaining teachers. This training included the exploration of democratic principles and collaboration techniques, and the importance of democratic relationships between supervisors and teachers was supported in an anthology of articles compiled by Robert R. Leeper (1969), then the director of the Association for Supervision and Curriculum Development and the editor of *Educational Leadership*.

New Models for Changing Times: Supervision from 1960 through the 1990s

The 1960s saw the rise of a novel type of supervision in a response to a number of factors, including the increasing size and complexity of the school organization;

new federal involvement through grants and programs; the rise of collective bargaining; an increase in teacher professional development opportunities as a result of Sputnik and the space race; and changes to new math, bilingual education, and other curriculum and instruction initiatives. Supervision in this era transformed to meet social needs, promoting individual respect for the supervisor, for the teacher, and, ultimately, for the learner.

One of the field's primary objectives became fostering leadership potential among teachers. As Pajak (1993) points out, the "teacher leadership" movement ironically faced adversity when another new development within the profession, collective bargaining, "effectively usurped the supervisor's traditional tools of group planning and problem solving. Teachers were no longer considered a source of creative ideas and solutions, but a problem of resistance that had to be overcome" (p. 5). Some believed collective bargaining principles effectively demoted teachers to a status similar to that of the 1800s, where they were expected to submit to authoritarian powers and conform for the good of the organization.

Let's pause now to take a closer look at three key developments that were especially critical in shaping supervision as the century came to a close: clinical supervision, the standards movement, and an increased focus on the learner.

The Introduction of Clinical Supervision

In the 1960s and 1970s, the authors of clinical supervision models refocused classroom learning and teaching by reintroducing democratic practices respectful of teachers. Morris Cogan (1973), a Harvard University professor considered to be the father of clinical supervision, proposed that supervision be a vehicle to disseminate pedagogical initiatives. He also suggested that teachers use self-analysis and self-direction while supervisors work in settings of face-to-face pre-conferences, classroom observations, and post-conferences. Robert Goldhammer (1969), Cogan's doctoral student, and Ralph Mosher and David Purpel (1972) emphasized teacher collegiality and self-supervision focusing on instructional strengths rather than deficiencies. Cogan and Goldhammer, especially, stressed that clinical approaches to supervision should be used only for the improvement of teaching and *not* for evaluation.

In his 1993 book *Approaches to Clinical Supervision,* Edward Pajak grouped clinical supervision models into four categories that reflected their basic tenets.

The first category of original clinical models (those of Cogan, Goldhammer, and Mosher and Purpel) was followed by a category that Pajak termed *humanistic/artistic* models, which included models proposed by Blumberg (1980) and Eisner (1982). In an environment of growing bureaucracy throughout the 1970s and 1980s, these models emphasized the establishment of trusting human relationships (Blumberg) and the development of teachers' unique talents (Eisner) as important for successful supervision. Thanks to the influence of these prominent researchers, strictly scientific approaches to supervision broadened to encourage the fostering of collegiality and personal concern. However, the 1980s rapidly shifted the emphasis of supervision back to task analysis, incorporating two more of Pajak's categories of clinical models: *technical/didactic* and *developmental/reflective*. These models took a more rational and scientific approach to examining and reflecting on teacher behavior related to student response.

Teaching Behavior and Student Response (1980s)

Madeline Hunter's (1980) supervision model kicked off the decade by encouraging supervisors to focus on teacher behavior as a direct influence on student response. Her recommendations and those of other contemporaneous researchers (Acheson & Gall, 1980; Glatthorn, 1984; McGreal, 1983) included revising teacher and supervisor training programs to incorporate learned, practiced, and perfected skills in pedagogy. The belief was that objective criteria of effective teaching *did* exist and were teachable.

Although this return to a scientific approach to supervision incorporated contemporary psychological research and technology, the procedures included the basic tenets of clinical and collegial methodology. The emphases on staff development and peer coaching were seen as viable means for improving teaching in order to improve learning (Joyce & Showers, 1988).

Pajak's final category of clinical models, *developmental/reflective models,* included the work of many researchers who emphasized that self-analysis and reflection on the part of teachers were critical to teaching success. This emphasis brought about the implementation of personal portfolios for professional growth.

Prominent individuals who conducted research during this time proposed that effective supervision requires understanding the developmental level of teachers regarding their decision making about teaching actions and student responses (Glickman, 1985) and emphasized the importance of teachers reflecting on and understanding the relationship between their teaching actions and their students' learning (Costa & Garmston, 1985, 1994). Both approaches require the supervisor to be aware of teachers' personal, humanistic concerns and take steps to guide teachers through reflective and decision-making processes that focus on the relationship between practices and student learning. Thus, light was beginning to shine on the essential need to consider the learner as a primary focus in both teaching and supervision.

A Focus on the Learner (The 1990s On)

The standards movement of the 1990s, designed to dramatically increase student and teacher accountability, should have profoundly affected supervision. Two national reports released in the 1980s, *A Nation at Risk: The Imperative for Educational Reform* (U.S. Department of Education National Commission on Excellence in Education, 1983) and *A Nation Prepared: Teachers for the 21st Century* (Carnegie Forum, 1986) blamed schools for mediocrity and called for increased student and teacher accountability. These reports fueled a national curriculum reform, signed into law by President Bill Clinton in 1994 under the name Goals 2000. Two of the six goals related directly to student performance:

> Goal 3: By the year 2000, American students will leave grades 4, 8, and 12 having demonstrated competency in challenging subject matter including English, mathematics, science, history and geography; and every school in America will ensure that all students learn to use their minds well, so they may be prepared for responsible citizenship, further learning, and productive employment in our modern economy.

> Goal 4: By the year 2000, U.S. students will be first in the world in science and mathematics. (U.S. Department of Education National Education Goals Panel, 1994, p. ix)

At the time, many agreed that education prior to the 1990s had been largely a process of intention with continued hope of improvement. This new definition required concrete results, demonstrated through student learning and evidenced through analyses of student learning data, and the preferred method of dealing with these data was through the creation of learning standards.

The standards-based curriculum movement that led states to develop standards documents and to No Child Left Behind's nationwide testing and accountability measures ushered in the 21st century. Varied efforts were made to minimize learning gaps, especially those between disadvantaged minority students and their peers; strengthen schools; and improve staff development. These efforts led to the frequent convening of professionals for the purpose of analyzing test data related to standards. Linda Law, director of secondary curriculum for New York's Baldwinsville School District observed:

> The data retreats, unfortunately, only confirmed what we already knew about student performance. Gathering educators into committees to view congeries of district test data did not provide a solution to fill the void between data and the improvement goal.
>
> We treated the data retreat as the solution; supervisors were called upon to inform teachers of progress or lack thereof. Looking back, we can see that supervisors did not have the training to act upon using the annual test results to reduce the gaps by changing classroom practices through supervision. We were not trained to improve the dialogue with teachers about teaching and learning. (Personal conversation with J. Pollock, 2007)

Ironically, these analyses of test data are conducted separately from classroom observations, in which supervisors use lengthy checklists to monitor teacher behaviors. The checklists conjure up memories of the rating scales prevalent in the early 1900s, the era of scientific management. And the message to supervisors—to determine the extent to which teachers comply with standards-based assessment—reminds us of efficiency language and unfavorable "inspection." The question educators must now ask is whether the requirement that principals first inspect the work of teachers to see if they are addressing standards in instructional planning and then infer that those who have done so have improved their students' learning until the test scores show differently has actually turned supervision back to what it was a century ago.

21st Century Models: Supervision for Improved Learning

The need to advance all students' learning, coupled with contemporary research findings about the power of instructional strategies and how critical feedback is to improving learning, leads us to the 21st century approach to elevating the importance of supervision.

Two noted works currently used by supervisors are *Enhancing Professional Practice: A Framework for Teaching* (Danielson, 2007) and *The Three-Minute Classroom Walk-Through: Changing School Supervisory Practice One Teacher at a Time* (Downey, Steffy, English, Frase, & Poston, 2004). Both approaches encourage principals to collaborate and help teachers learn how to reflect upon their own professional practice. Both stress the importance of improving teaching to improve learning. However, the process of analyzing data in these and other learning-centered approaches to supervision (Aseltine, Faryniarz, & Rigazio-DeGilio, 2006; Tucker & Stronge, 2005) primarily uses summative student data rather than a formative approach that concurrently analyzes student learning progress and teaching practices on a lesson-by-lesson basis.

Although standards-based supervision discussions are becoming more widespread, it is usually periodic performance indicators that define student learning. Too often, a final test result or a final subjective grade is used to report student achievement, with the student often unaware of learning progress until that final assessment is announced.

A Supervisory Tool to Improve Learning

We asked the question earlier in this chapter of why supervisory visits to classrooms are often dreaded and seen as occasional events of perfunctory judgment. What we didn't state is that supervisory visits to classrooms may be just as uncomfortable for supervisors as they are for teachers. What teachers and supervisors sometimes forget is that they share the same primary goal: to improve student learning. Teachers must believe supervisors are not in their classrooms to "inspect" them, and supervisors must be equipped with the tools they need to give teachers accurate, helpful feedback that will support sound, formative instructional decision making. If these components of the supervision process are not in place, then a disconnect occurs that fosters resentment on the part of teachers and unwelcome feelings (at best) or feelings of failure (at worst) on the part of supervisors.

We can see that the role of supervision in our country's history has progressed from oversight to collaboration, despite some stagnations or even reversals along the way. We have moved from inspection to the use of rating scales designed to promote organizational efficiency, to the inclusion of democratic and cooperative approaches, and back to a form of rating and inspection through standards-based criteria checklists. While the primary goal of supervision is improving student achievement, the focus of supervision has changed from the organization itself to teacher learning and finally, now, to student learning.

We believe that the supervisory structure discussed in this book and based on the Teaching Schema for Master Learners allows a teacher and supervisor to cooperatively apply scientific principles about student learning. Supervisors can share in improving student learning by observing critical decisions that teachers make during their teaching, cooperating in planning and reflecting upon those decisions, and using classroom and test data to determine effectiveness and make changes. The tools and approaches we discuss in this book can be used in a clinical approach, with pre-conferences, classroom observations, and post-conferences. The Schema includes specific, sequenced steps that encourage reflection and professional development. In other words, it will complement, not replace, most existing supervisory models.

A critical component that separates our proposed supervisory approach from others is that we encourage daily, ongoing feedback from teachers to students about students' learning progress; it is important that this feedback be tied to lesson goals and objectives. Teachers' pedagogical decisions affect students' classroom performance and achievement gains on a daily basis. Effective supervisory work with teachers examines this influence and determines how to use daily progress in student learning to inform teaching decisions.

Supervision in the latter decades of the 20th century primarily focused on teacher behaviors, assuming that if instruction improved, student learning would likewise improve. A closer look at student achievement data reveals the flaw in this axiom. However, the research about learning indicates that a supervisor can take a pivotal role in ensuring that students learn. Supervision that includes useful feedback to teachers and assists teachers in providing frequent and useful feedback to students contributes greatly to improved student achievement. The supervisor's role is to implement effective tools in coaching and to work cooperatively with teachers to make decisions based on researched pedagogical practices. The Teaching Schema for Master Learners—specifically, each of its components, referred to as GANAG—is such a tool.

Supervisor Voice

Richard Zimman, Superintendent

Based on his experiences as a teacher and district leader, Richard tells about how he transformed his own thinking about teacher evaluation and supervision and discusses how his district changed its culture for the better by improving learning through supervision.

Here We Go Again: Observing and Evaluating

"The next item on our agenda is teacher observation and evaluation," I announced to the district's administrative team gathered for one of our regular meetings. The friendly banter that characterized our close-knit team stopped, as if a person we were talking about had just entered the room. Everyone suddenly showed intense interest in his or her shoes or the paperwork in front of them. No one was making eye contact with me or with one another.

I wasn't surprised at all by the staff's reaction. Teacher observation and evaluation—even discussing teacher observation and evaluation—is the third rail of education administration; no one wants to touch it. After nearly 20 years of administration in three different school districts, I had a good idea why. Almost universally, observation and evaluation were seen as processes that gobbled huge amounts of time and effort without making significant differences in teacher performance, student achievement, or organizational culture. Two personal examples from my own career help to illustrate why this point of view is so widespread.

The first incident dates to my time teaching high school, when our building administrator incorporated a flashcard quiz on the components of the Madeline Hunter model into our pre-observation conferences. Although we understood that the principal had good intentions and just wanted to raise the level of understanding and discourse regarding lesson design, the absurdity of using flashcards to achieve that higher level provided much fodder for teachers lounge spoofs, which undermined a positive organizational culture.

A second example comes from another district, where the superintendent launched an initiative to improve teaching by adopting a reflective supervisory model based on well-established research. Much time and expense went into training administrators to use this model. Principals spent many hours observing each teacher and engaging in reflective conferences. A four-point evaluation scale was developed and applied to the summative evaluations and then totaled so that district administrators could discern trends and gaps that would guide future districtwide staff development efforts. Additional time and expense went to training all teachers on how to use the model to guide their practice. The net result was more paperwork, more meetings, and more analysis . . . but, unfortunately, no significant differences in teaching or student achievement and no organizational shift to more reflective practice.

These scenarios were swirling through my head as I looked around the table at my administrative team. I knew what they were thinking, and they knew that I knew, but nobody wanted to say it out loud. The collective, if unspoken, voice of experience told us all the same thing: "Buckle up, because here we go again."

A Dedicated Focus on Teachers Is Not Enough

About 15 years prior to the meeting I've described, a joint teacher–administrator committee in our district had developed a teacher supervision system with much fanfare. It was a clinical model similar to the Danielson model (2007), and its focus was having each teacher demonstrate various competencies while planning, teaching, and engaging in professional practice. There was an ongoing tug-of-war between teachers who believed that they had exceeded the performance standards (the "walk on water" descriptor) and administrators who were trying to provide honest feedback without making the teaching staff feel unappreciated. It was a very time-consuming task that, in the best-case scenario, left teachers feeling like they put in a lot of effort only to be told that they were good teachers—which everyone already knew. In the more prevalent scenario, less-than-glowing feedback triggered teacher resentment and frustration that tended to fester into feelings of being underappreciated. The end result? The process didn't improve teacher instructional prowess, it didn't improve student achievement, and it made building a positive school culture impossible.

All this was in my mind when I put the topic of teacher observation and evaluation on the agenda for the administrative team meeting. For one thing, I wanted to ensure that the system we were using was consistently implemented districtwide. Because the district practice is to route all summative evaluations through the superintendent's office, I had read them all prior to their being filed away in the district's official personnel files, and I had noticed considerable differences in the way that our administrators approached the evaluation process. Somehow, I thought that getting all the principals on the same page would make a positive difference, and to do that, we had to discuss how each administrator was interpreting and approaching his or her observations, evaluations, and ratings.

I was intrigued by the summative report format that one principal used. It consisted of a summary of the teacher's skills in targeted areas, followed by a brief list of suggestions for improvement based on the rating components of the evaluation instrument. For probationary teachers, this feedback provided some direction for their own development and set benchmarks for retaining their jobs. For veteran teachers, this feedback was a relatively benign way of pointing out a few areas for professional growth. We decided to adopt this format for summative reports on teacher observations.

How did that work out? Some teachers readily accepted the feedback and sought ways to improve in the designated areas. More often, though, teachers either argued that they were already "outstanding" in those areas or set about to prove the principal wrong by showering him or her with artifacts, parental letters of praise, or classroom activities to which the principal was invited. Well, I thought, at least now we're talking about instruction instead of simply filling out forms in ways that attempt to avoid making anyone uncomfortable. But clearly, this focus on teachers and their instruction just wasn't enough.

Working Hard, but Stuck

Our district curriculum was written and comprehensive, but the content was still a hodgepodge of activities, textbook chapter titles, state standards, and power standards. By trying to include everyone's interests, the curriculum had evolved without a guiding principle to provide clarity of purpose about student learning. In other words, the curriculum offered little guidance for focused classroom instruction, leaving teachers to think in terms of stringing together activities and worksheets for days until it was time for a test.

Instructional practices in our district ran the gamut from inquiry approach to direct instruction, depending upon the teacher's preferences for delivery. Because the district is in a college community, there is a strong undercurrent of academic freedom within K–12 classrooms. Our schools truly resembled the cliché of a group of independent educational entrepreneurs sharing a common parking lot. Without a districtwide instructional model, there was no common language, so collegial discussions about instructional practices were difficult to have with any regularity or sustainability. There were no data-based decisions about which instructional practices should be used for which content and which students. Teachers were working very hard, but the district's shotgun approach to instruction kept those efforts from being as effective as they should have been. For maximum impact, we needed a common instructional model using a benchmark-based curriculum.

Our assessment practices were another example of too much effort with insufficient results. To encourage teachers to move toward the "assessment for learning" approach fostered by No Child Left Behind, our district had established exit-outcome learning targets for each grade level and subject area. Teacher-developed target assessments were administered at least three times a year to gather data for instructional planning, but the process was regarded by many as an extraneous administrative mandate rather than a useful tool for increasing student learning. A better solution would be an assessment process that integrated research-based instruction, with the instructional process firmly rooted in a benchmark-based curriculum.

Although our teachers typically recorded many grades for student assignments and tests, the post-mortem compilation of all the student's struggles and successes into a single letter or number grade didn't really provide any useful information to the student (or parent or future teacher) about what the student needed to study further. The result was a constant flow of information from teachers to students and parents that was little more than a scorecard, when what was *really* needed were coaching tips, strategies, and practice regimens.

Our district had begun participating in a series of workshops based on *Improving Student Learning One Teacher at a Time* (Pollock, 2007), and our teachers were becoming more comfortable with the Big Four approach, which included intense reviews of our assessment and student feedback practices. We were focusing staff development on research-based instructional practices, especially those presented in *Classroom Instruction That Works* (Marzano et al., 2001). So, positive changes were beginning to happen, yet something was missing: the connecting piece that would tie it all together and move our classrooms to the next level.

A "World-Changing" Shift Through a Focus on Learning

Still searching optimistically and believing in the power of collaboration and the development of a positive team culture, I registered our administrative team for a workshop. Jane E. Pollock began the course by reviewing the concepts of the Big Four approach from *Improving Student Learning One Teacher at a Time*, but she moved quickly to using the Teaching Schema for Master Learners as a tool for administrators. I was skeptical, having survived several other presentations on lesson design templates in my career. Yet the more Jane explained the historical and research underpinnings of the Schema and how it integrated with the Big Four, the clearer it was that this approach could weave together our initiatives and might actually improve student achievement. As we reviewed the status of each of the Big Four components in our district and how using the Schema as supervisors would affect us, our entire administrative team recognized that our world had just shifted.

Enjoying More Success with the Schema

The Teaching Schema for Master Learners, specifically the Schema's sequenced steps referred to as GANAG, became the foundation for our student achievement and school improvement efforts:

• It called for clear lesson goals, so our curriculum now had to identify benchmarks and content objectives for each grade level and subject area.

• It called for research-based instructional strategies that adhered to lesson time frames, so our teacher observation and evaluation system was revised to include the Schema.

• It called for teachers to assess student learning, so we began to revise target assessments and performance assessment practices in order to deliver subsequent lessons that were more focused on areas of need.

• Finally, it called for ongoing coaching feedback, so we began to grade by benchmarks.

In summary, GANAG touches all aspects of the Big Four in every classroom and provides an overriding connection among all aspects of teaching and learning. And what's more, it emphasizes that teachers should know their content areas deeply and urges them to maintain autonomy over pedagogical practices.

This is not to say that our work is done and our district is now on cruise control. But we have a unifying structure and a destination that everyone knows and understands. How did we proceed after Jane's workshop series concluded? Some principals talked with individual teachers about the Schema. Other principals shared a brief introduction to it with their entire faculty.

The planning began with the district's teacher observation and evaluation committee. The Schema was inserted into a revised system that used a modified Pathwise approach (Danielson, 2007). Pre-observation conferences, lesson observations, and post-observation conferences would now include GANAG planning, data collection, and analysis. Reflection would be based, in part, on thinking about the lesson in terms of the Teaching Schema for Master Learners.

Next, we needed a plan to merge Schema in-service training with a presentation regarding the district's revised observation and evaluation document and procedure. Instead of being separate, the Schema was now part of the district's expectations for teachers as well as part of their performance evaluation. Staff development days immediately preceding the new school year featured a half-day session for all faculty members, put together by the district committee for teacher observation and evaluation. Teachers and administrators from the committee supplied everyone with perspectives from both the teacher and administrator viewpoints. In addition, the information was presented using an integrated approach that demonstrated how the Big Four, the Schema, and the modified Pathwise evaluation system reinforced one another in a cohesive, districtwide model that would increase teacher effectiveness and student achievement.

The Schema's Ripple Effect

As the year progressed, our district began to see evidence of the pervasive ripple effect of the Teaching Schema for Master Learners. A few teachers in each school began talking about modifying curriculum to reflect a shift to focused benchmarks and content objectives so that they could better implement GANAG in their lessons. Some began revising their instruction and designing more purposeful lessons using research-based instructional strategies. Some began to revise their assessment practices in order to better understand the mastery level of their students. And a few teachers began new feedback practices based on the Schema by experimenting with grading by benchmarks.

We've recognized that each teacher is different, following a different path to instructional improvement. We see the process as akin to tackling a jigsaw puzzle; there are many pieces to put together before the big picture is clear, and teachers need to determine the best sequence for themselves. However, unlike our pre-GANAG days, when every teacher was completing a different picture, we now all use GANAG to work toward the same picture, shaping and weaving together the Big Four components. For students, who pass through numerous teachers during their K–12 years, the Teaching Schema for Master Learners provides a consistent approach and a cohesive learning framework. For teachers, whose classrooms are full of students who had different teachers the previous year, the Schema furnishes an articulated approach and common language that increases collegiality and effectiveness. And for administrators, the Schema has transformed supervision of instruction from a dreaded task to a worthwhile one that actually results in better teaching and increased learning. It all begins with one teacher and one principal at a time.

2

Supervision and the Teaching Schema for Master Learners

After reading this chapter, you should be able to

• Explain how a principal can guide a teacher using the basic tenets of the Big Four.

• Describe the Teaching Schema for Master Learners as a conversation guide for principals and teachers focusing on planning and assessment.

• Understand the critical importance of ongoing feedback to both teachers and students.

IN A BOOK TITLED *BETTER: A SURGEON'S NOTES ON PERFORMANCE*, SURGEON ATUL Gawande (2007) writes about cases in which failure to follow basic medical practices compromises the physician's oath to reduce patient pain and mortality. For example, since the mid-1800s, members of the medical profession have recognized hand washing as an effective way to prevent infection and thus reduce pain and mortality. Even so, Gawande reports, hospital employees have astonishingly low compliance rates with hand washing guidelines. Despite "knowing better," these medical personnel systematically neglect a well-known, research-verified practice that "makes patients better." There's an analogy to be drawn between the physician's oath and our oath, as educators, to improve student learning. Is there a technique or research-based finding that we *know* improves learning but that we must learn or be reminded to apply conscientiously and systematically? We say yes. It is feedback.

Good feedback is a direct means through which today's principals can help students (and teachers) do "better" in school. This entails (1) providing teachers with feedback on instructional decision making and delivery, based on classroom observation, and (2) explicitly helping teachers improve the quality of verbal or nonverbal, written, and recorded or reported feedback they provide to their students. Feedback to teachers that is specifically targeted to planning, instructing, and assessing, rather than being only complimentary praise, is a golden key to fostering cooperative work with teachers that results in improved student learning.

At the end of the previous chapter, we recommended that principals keep many of their current supervisory and evaluation practices intact but adapt their models, where appropriate, to incorporate aspects of the Big Four and, more specifically, the Teaching Schema for Master Learners. For supervisors—be they principals or coaches—using the Schema to discuss classroom activities with teachers leads to clearer communication about solutions for improving student learning by improving teaching methods.

Guiding Teachers to Guide Students to Better Learning

Improving Student Learning One Teacher at a Time (Pollock, 2007) describes the Big Four, four elements of teaching that can be deliberately modified to energize teaching, improve student learning, and galvanize effective program change. Once again, the tenets of the Big Four are as follows:

1. *Use a well-articulated curriculum.* Institute clearly articulated, "just-right" grade-level curriculum standards (benchmarks).

2. *Plan for delivery.* Plan and deliver instruction using the Teaching Schema for Master Learners with research-based strategies.

3. *Vary assessment.* Assessment methods should cover a wide range and should include frequent formative as well as summative assessment practices.

4. *Give criterion-based feedback.* Revitalize feedback methods, including scoring to benchmarks in grade books and generating reports (such as report cards) that more accurately inform students, parents or guardians, and team members about student progress.

None of these tenets is new to educators. What *is* new, however, is the idea of taking them together as a system of connecting parts rather than as separate tasks with separate staff development initiatives. The Big Four approach merges the well-known triad of curriculum, instruction, and assessment with a contemporary emphasis on purposeful feedback to the student, and it is the dynamic interaction of the four that results in better learning. And, as we'll illustrate shortly, the Schema provides a way to ensure the inclusion of each of the Big Four's tenets into every lesson.

All four tenets of the Big Four can affect teaching on a daily basis; however, components 2 and 3 unite the supervisory tasks of conferencing and observing classroom teaching directly with the acts of planning and assessment to generate better student results. The "planning for delivery" component (referred to as the Schema) provides teachers with a sequence for mapping out their instruction; the "varying assessment" component emphasizes giving students formative feedback about their progress on grade-level curriculum standards (benchmarks), as well as designing different types of tasks. A principal who deliberately connects post-observation conferencing with these two aspects of teaching is more likely to make the leap from improving teaching to also improving learning.

Researchers argue that better feedback to the learner results in better student performance (Hattie & Timperley, 2007; Marzano et al., 2001). However, merely fine-tuning feedback strategies may not bring about desired gains. Feedback that is based on a weak set of learning targets may not improve communication or performance; likewise, increased feedback focused only on task completion will not increase knowledge retention and application. The Big Four approach emphasizes the importance of criterion-based feedback; the better the learning targets, the more useful the criterion-based feedback to the recipient.

Principals can affect learning in a meaningful way by using the Schema to guide their dialogue with teachers during pre- and post-observation conferences. By focusing supervisory feedback on the components of the Schema, principals can best ensure each teacher structures and delivers lessons that will lead students to meaningful, lasting learning.

Not surprisingly, many principals introduce the Big Four concepts and the Schema to their faculties because they sincerely wish to improve individual student learning; however, the principal's role in the Big Four approach is not overtly defined. For example, Jim Perkins, an elementary principal at Gunnison Community School, encouraged teachers to assess themselves on the Big Four and participate in professional development, but he also contended that while his evaluation model was working to document the work of teachers as employees, he would need to redefine his supervision model to help teachers improve student learning.

When Jim attended a seminar about the Big Four with his teaching faculty, he asked, "Can I just embed the Teaching Schema for Master Learners from the Big Four into the classroom observation form I am using now? That way, my conversation with teachers could align directly with their preparation, and we could focus our pre- and post-conversations deliberately on student performance." Jim's revised pre-observation form is shown in Figure 2.1.

Jim certainly intended to improve teaching as the means to improve learning, but he wanted to go about it by improving his supervision: collaborating with teachers to produce better instruction and assessment. In other words, he wanted to be sure that the work he was doing to support teachers would really translate into student achievement.

The Teaching Schema for Master Learners . . . and Supervisors

The Teaching Schema for Master Learners includes the following steps, presented here in a slightly different way than in this book's Introduction:

> G: Set the learning **GOAL**/benchmark or objective
> *Opportunity for feedback*
> A: **ACCESS** prior student knowledge
> *Opportunity for feedback*
> N: Acquire **NEW INFORMATION**—declarative, procedural, or both
> *Opportunity for feedback*
> A: **APPLY** a thinking skill or use knowledge in a new situation
> *Opportunity for feedback*
> G: **GENERALIZE** or summarize knowledge learned

In addition to these steps, teachers can assign *homework,* if necessary (as Step 6), and *assessment tasks,* including quizzes, tests, or common assessments, as needed. Note that throughout the process, after each step, teachers are prompted

---

FIGURE 2.1
Gunnison Community School Pre-Observation Form

Teacher: _____   Date: _____

Date of observation: _____   Time: _____

1. How would you like me to observe and provide feedback to you? What do you want me to look for?

2. Will this be new teaching or review?

3. What materials will be needed?

4. What are the benchmarks/objectives to be taught and assessed?

5. How will you access prior knowledge?

6. What is the new information to be taught?

7. What is the application (thinking skill or real-world situation)?

8. How will you assess student learning?

9. Describe the strategy for generalization or summary.

10. What will extend the day (homework)?

Please attach a copy of your lesson plan, assessment instruments for the lesson, seating chart, handouts, etc.

Source: James R. Perkins, Gunnison Community School, Gunnison, Colorado.

to incorporate *feedback* to students so that they can make improvements in their learning.

We recommend that principals use the Schema during their classroom observations and as a discussion frame for conferencing with teachers before and after. Many principals embed the steps (G-A-N-A-G) in existing observation forms, as Jim Perkins does, thereby explicitly concentrating the dialogue about student performance as a common goal for supervisors and teachers and guiding the collaborative exchange of ideas between supervisor and teacher so that reflecting on and making decisions about teaching practices directly affects student achievement of curriculum targets. Although not all students may meet standards set for performance on curriculum benchmarks, teachers and supervisors can more genuinely share the planning for making necessary changes in instruction, program, or resources to produce student results.

In the remainder of this chapter, we provide an overview of the ways teachers might use the GANAG steps of the Schema for lesson design. It's an approach that organizes the lesson around the learner's learning, not around activities alone. Subsequent chapters describe how supervisors can evaluate lessons guided by the Schema and how they should provide instructional feedback to teachers.

Lesson Design Using the Schema

Each lesson begins by identifying the grade-level curriculum standards (G). Jane and her colleagues, in *Classroom Instruction That Works* (Marzano et al., 2001), stated that setting objectives and providing feedback to the learner using those objectives is one of nine critical strategies for improving learning. In order to provide verbal, nonverbal, and written feedback to students throughout the class period to help them progress toward learning the grade-level curriculum standards (benchmarks), the beginning of a lesson should establish the opportunity for self-assessment, peer assessment, and expert or teacher assessment. When working with teachers, we remind them that if they do not clearly identify the content targets for a lesson, students will set their own—and these are unlikely to relate to math, music, or mythology. Neurologist and educator Judy Willis (2006) writes that when students are prompted to know what to expect, the "result is greater attention, connection, and memory retention" (p. 41).

After setting the goal (G), the teacher should help students "fire their neurons" by using strategies such as physical representations, open-ended questions, cues, or novelty to engage them and prepare them for the learning ahead; we call this process "accessing prior student knowledge" (A). Engaging students to learn or make memories requires capturing their attention. David Ghoogasian, a brain-based learning scholar, reminds us that when a student pays attention to a cue, pathways in the brain are activated, focused, and strengthened, making them stronger and more efficient at transporting data into long-term memory (personal conversation with J. Pollock, 2007). Stated differently, new information can be more meaningful to students if they connect to it and create associations with it; otherwise, the new information is at risk of being discarded or eliminated. Ghoogasian also suggests that the brain needs a certain level of emotion for optimal learning to occur, so using strategies to make personal connections through brainstorming, reciprocal teaching, or analogies can help the learner make emotional connections stronger.

With teachers, we refer to accessing prior student knowledge as the time when a teacher directs students to open metaphoric "tabs on the folders." If we can predict that a student has a "folder" for a topic, even if this understanding is puny or mistaken, we increase our chances for enabling the student to organize, practice, and store new information.

Once learners are "neurologically connected," the teacher can present new information (N) and opportunities for students to gather, organize, and practice that information. Processing new information looks different depending on whether one retains the knowledge in declarative or procedural memory. Information can be factual and conceptual, such as that learned in a typical social studies class, or can involve the steps of a procedure, or habitual knowledge, such as in a math class. Generally, students need guidance and instruction on how to organize factual information. Students can also be taught thinking skills to apply (A) or present original ideas. Similarly, students can view demonstrations of steps in procedures and practice these steps with corrective feedback to reach a level of independence and proficiency.

Throughout the lesson, the teacher should deliberately plan various opportunities to ensure that students receive feedback (from the teacher, from peers, or through reflection) about how well they are learning the new information. When the grade-level curriculum standards (benchmarks) are clearly stated, the teacher can constantly manage the activity to include verbal and nonverbal, written, and scored opportunities for learners to review their own progress toward meeting the targets. The techniques for providing formative feedback to learners require the teacher to share learning goals with the learners and also to implement various teaching strategies to "check for understanding." In subsequent chapters, we cite different options principals can suggest to teachers.

At the end of the lesson, equipped with new knowledge, learners generalize (G) or summarize their understandings by writing a journal note, sharing verbally with peers, or using other ways to indicate what they know and how well they know it. Willis (2006) calls the process of tying the ending of a lesson back to the beginning a "dendrite food, because it makes new learning connections that can grow into more dendrites" (p. 86). This self-regulating skill of metacognitively drawing a conclusion, checking for progress, and readjusting the degree of goal progress contributes to learners' iterative nature; that is, it motivates them to return the next day for further instruction.

Terese Weiler, at Traeger Elementary School, described to us how planning lessons using the Schema (what she and her colleagues call "GANAG-ing"—it rhymes with "unflagging") has improved their attention to students' academic needs and personal learning behaviors, as well as providing a structure for generating useful and provocative feedback. Teachers portray the Schema as being flexible enough to use at most grade levels and with most subject areas.

A number of principals have adapted their observation forms to include the Schema but retain the district-specific variations that are important for them to use. Rubicon School District Superintendent Dan Hanrahan, also principal of Saylesville School, complemented a lesson design template that he recommended to teachers (Figure 2.2) with a classroom observation form (Figure 2.3). Similarly, Superintendent Susan Alexander from Markesan Schools designed a Schema-informed district observation form for K–12 principals (Figure 2.4) that also incorporates other districtwide initiatives—in this case, use of effective instructional strategies.

In addition, teachers explain that when their principals visit their classrooms, they can adapt the Schema to include new instructional strategies they learn from supervisory visits. In an effort to focus lesson discussion on the learners, teacher Kathy Mohr and instructional technology specialist Diane Quirk designed a lesson template around the Schema that the principal could use as well. Kathy wanted the feedback about her lesson to be directly aligned to how she viewed the sequence of steps and the guided learning, so she asked

FIGURE 2.2

Saylesville School Lesson Plan Template

Teacher: _____   Grade: _____   Date: _____

Standard/Benchmark:

Goal: What will you be teaching? What is it that you want students to know, be like, or be able to do? How will you communicate the learning goal to students?

Accessing **Prior Knowledge:** What will you do to access students' prior knowledge?

New Information: What is the new, important declarative and procedural knowledge that students must learn to achieve the goal of this lesson?

Apply Knowledge: How will you present the new information multiple times, using a variety of input modes?

Content Chunks: How will you divide and teach the content to engage students' brains?

Generalization/Summary: How will students summarize the learning in relation to the lesson goal? How will they develop their own generalizations? How will *you* know that *they* know?

FEEDBACK

FEEDBACK

FEEDBACK

Assessment (Traditional/Authentic): How will you know students have learned the content, via a variety of assessment modalities? How will you document this over time?

Materials/Technologies: What materials and/or technologies will you need to present this lesson?

Source: Daniel J. Hanrahan, Rubicon School District, Rubicon, Wisconsin.

FIGURE 2.3

Excerpt of the Saylesville School Classroom Observation Form

Today's Date: _____   Teacher: _____

Unit/Lesson Name and Number:_____   Grade Level: _____

Length of Class Period:_____   No. of Students Present in the Class: _____

Pre-observation Date (if applicable): _____   Post-observation Date: _____

Formative Lesson Assessment

Goal Setting/Lesson Purpose
1. How clearly (comprehensively) was the lesson purpose communicated?
   (Please circle one number)

   Not clear |___|___|___|___|___|___| Very clear
        1 2 3 4 5 6 7

2. The teacher clearly demonstrated understanding of the purpose of the lesson by how she/he responded to questions: Yes / No

3. The students demonstrated understanding of the purpose of the lesson by their interaction and questions: Yes / No

4. The students were provided feedback on their understanding of the lesson goal: Yes / No

Comments:

Accessing Prior Knowledge
1. How effectively did the teacher access students' prior knowledge?

   Not clear |___|___|___|___|___|___| Very clear
        1 2 3 4 5 6 7

2. The students were provided feedback on their expression of prior knowledge as it relates to the goal: Yes / No

Comments:

Source: Daniel J. Hanrahan, Rubicon School District, Rubicon, Wisconsin.

FIGURE 2.4
Markesan Schools Classroom Observation Form

Teacher: _____ Class: _____ Observer: _____ Date: _____

Goal/Objective Set/Connection to Benchmarks: | **Comments:**

☐	Students understand what they will be learning
☐	Students know what makes good work
☐	Lesson/activities related to benchmarks
☐	

Access Prior Knowledge: | **Comments:**

☐	Reviewing text, passages, problems or content
☐	Activation of prior knowledge
☐	Purposeful set, focused activities
☐	

New Information Input:

Procedural: | **Comments:**

☐	Steps or processes comprehended by students
☐	Expectation of skills introduced
☐	Guided practice
☐	

Declarative: | **Comments:**

☐	Structured note taking
☐	Clarifying/organizing ideas
☐	Vocabulary development
☐	

Application/Use: | **Comments:**

☐	Engagement of students on task
☐	Clear instructions given
☐	Use of assessment to guide instruction
☐	

FIGURE 2.4

Markesan Schools Classroom Observation Form *(continued)*

Teacher: _____   Class: _____   Observer: _____   Date: _____

Generalizing/Closure: **Comments:**

☐	Effective use of instructional time
☐	Monitors student work
☐	Students can articulate what they have learned
☐	

Evidence of Instructional Strategies Throughout Lesson: **Comments:**

☐	Identifying similarities and differences
☐	Summarizing and note taking
☐	Reinforcing effort and providing recognition
☐	Homework and practice
☐	Nonlinguistic representations (graphic organizers, models, maps)
☐	Cooperative learning
☐	Setting objectives and providing feedback
☐	Generating and testing hypotheses or problem solving
☐	Questions, cues, advanced organizers

General Comments:

Source: Susan H. Alexander, Markesan District Schools, Markesan, Wisconsin.

Diane to help her create both a teacher version and a supervisor's note-taking version. We have included an example of both forms in Figures 2.5 and 2.6.

Feedback Works

To supervisors, then, the Schema provides the blueprint for learning for a class of students. Just as a prospective landowner might peruse a real estate map of building lots, the principal uses the language of the Schema steps in a pre-observation conference to get the "lay of the land"; later, GANAG can guide the principal through the lesson and provides the map or discussion frame for giving feedback to teachers to make improvements for learning. If the teacher uses the Schema to plan the lesson, the pre- and post-observation conversations create strong links between the principal, the teacher, student learning, and curriculum results.

Aiming at improved student performance as the common goal for supervisors and teachers is a refreshing addition to supervision models. When we studied the history of supervision, we noticed that in most supervision models, the supervisor primarily focused on teaching practices, tacitly assuming that teaching, if done well, would automatically translate into greater student achievement. Alternatively, when the supervisors watched for student behaviors in relation to teaching behaviors, they tended to look at literally defined behavior, rather than at cognitively based performance on curriculum targets. This was likely due to specificity at the time that defined curriculum targets as being behavioral objectives, outcomes, or even test results.

In the 20th century, feedback about teaching decisions and behaviors became a pronounced feature of most supervision models. The Teaching Schema for Master Learners supports a supervisor in providing feedback about how teaching practices affect individual student achievement on curriculum targets. This is different from providing feedback to teachers about how practices affect classes as a whole and how teachers can become master teachers. In addition, we recommend that the teacher and principal discuss student learning that is visible during the lesson observation—learning that is ongoing—and how that daily performance ties to common assessments, tests, or summative data analyzed at the end of a term. The principal and teacher should discuss the grade book (scored or graded performance trends) as well as the plan book (lesson plans).

FIGURE 2.5

Teacher Version of Lesson Plan Template

Subject: 6th Grade English/Language Arts
Benchmarks: LA6.3.2—Defines, identifies, and uses parts of speech in writing; LA6.3.5—Uses conventions of punctuation
Materials:

Schema	Classroom Activities	Additional Comments
Set the Goal	Students will be able to express how to use an apostrophe to show possession in their own writing. Students will be able to write two sentences with the same words, one with an apostrophe, one without. The students will accompany the sentences with pictures expressing the importance of apostrophes.	In their spirals, students will revise the teacher's goals into "I" statements. (Example: "I will be able to say in my own words how to use an apostrophe to show possession." "I will be able to come up with an example of two sentences in which the apostrophe matters.") Students will return to these goals at the end of the lesson. They will answer in writing whether they met their goal, or if they did not, what strategy they will use in order to meet their goal.
Access Prior Knowledge	Read *The Girl's Like Spaghetti: Why, You Can't Manage Without Apostrophes!* by Lynne Truss	When examining the illustrations in this book, students will begin to hear and see the importance of the part of speech we call an apostrophe.
Acquire New Information	Teacher will display transparency and review the characteristics of a possessive noun. Teacher will discuss what possession/ownership means and differentiate between plural and possessive. Teacher will display examples from the book read during the APK activity on the overhead and point out the differences. This will allow for additional time to grasp the concepts and for a visual aid.	First, teacher may wish to review what common and proper nouns are. Whiteboards may be used for immediate feedback; assessment informs teacher whether students are ready to move on.
Apply Knowledge	Students will design their own two sentences, one with an apostrophe and one without. They will be able to express the difference between plural, possessive, and plural-possessive. Students will also draw two pictures expressing the difference between the two sentences.	Students' work will be displayed so the other students can see their work as more examples of the same concept; students share comments on examples with one another.
Generalize or Summarize Knowledge Learned	Students will use whiteboards to answer questions regarding possessive, plural, and plural-possessive posed on the overhead. Students will share with a partner what a difference an apostrophe makes. Students will then write a noun that can be changed by an apostrophe.	This will allow students a chance to summarize and provide the teacher an immediate assessment.
Assessment	Grammar assessment: Students will have opportunities to work on this assignment during study hall, after school, and at home.	Teacher will observe students to determine if they need extra examples or assistance.

Source: Kathleen M. Mohr, Ray Middle School, Baldwinsville, New York.

FIGURE 2.6

Supervisor Version of the Observation Template

Subject: 6th Grade English/Language Arts

Teacher: Kathy Mohr, Ray Middle School

Benchmarks: LA6.3.2 – Defines, identifies, and uses parts of speech in writing
LA6.3.5 – Uses conventions of punctuation

Materials:

Schema	Classroom Activities	Additional Comments	Observation	Comments
Set the Goal	Students will be able to express how to use an apostrophe to show possession in their own writing. Students will be able to write two sentences with the same words, one with an apostrophe, one without. The students will accompany the sentences with pictures expressing the importance of apostrophes.	In their spirals, students will revise the teacher's goals into "I" statements. (Example: "I will be able to say in my own words how to use an apostrophe to show possession.") Students will return to these goals at the end of the lesson. They will answer in writing whether they met their goal, or if they did not, what strategy they will use in order to meet their goal.	*Administrator writes what took place during the actual lesson*	*Administrator notes questions/comments about this portion of the lesson*
Access Prior Student Knowledge	Read *The Girl's Like Spaghetti: Why, You Can't Manage Without Apostrophes!* by Lynne Truss	When examining the illustrations in this book, students will begin to hear and see the importance of the part of speech we call an apostrophe.		

Acquire New Information	Teacher will display transparency and review the characteristics of a possessive noun. Teacher will discuss what possession/ownership means and differentiate between plural and possessive. Teacher will display examples from the book read during the APK activity on the overhead and point out the differences. This will allow for additional time to grasp the concepts and for a visual aid.	First, teacher may wish to review what common and proper nouns are. Whiteboards may be used for immediate feedback; assessment informs teacher whether students are ready to move on.
Apply Knowledge	Students will design their own two sentences, one with an apostrophe and one without. They will be able to express the difference between plural, possessive, and plural-possessive. Students will also draw two pictures expressing the difference between the two sentences.	Students' work will be displayed so the other students can see their work as more examples of the same concept; students share comments on examples with one another.
Generalize or Summarize Knowledge Learned	Students will use whiteboards to answer questions regarding possessive, plural, and plural-possessive posed on the overhead. Students will then share with a partner at their table what a difference an apostrophe makes. Students will then write a noun on the whiteboard that can be changed by an apostrophe.	This will allow not only for a chance for the students to summarize but also for an immediate assessment for the teacher.
Assessment	Grammar assessment: Applications/assessments will not be due at the end of class. Students will have opportunities to work on this assignment during study hall, extended-core, and after school. They will also be able to bring work home.	Teacher will observe students to determine if they need extra examples or assistance.

Source: Kathleen M. Mohr, Ray Middle School, Baldwinsville, New York.

The most significant concept of the Teaching Schema for Master Learners is that feedback—ongoing, explicit, and focused on reasonable learning targets—improves learning for students and for teachers, too. Most principals using the Schema think of "feedback" not as summative in nature, but as a formative tool used for improvement on a daily basis. We conclude that adding the Schema with the "double dose of feedback" (for teachers and for students) to the supervisor's classroom observation is a manageable change to existing evaluation or supervisory procedures, and a change that directly affects student learning.

The Rest of the Big Four

We note that the primary responsibility for the first component of the Big Four approach—drafting and editing curriculum (or learning) targets—could continue to be a centralized districtwide or schoolwide curriculum process. The revision of benchmarks and programs by the curriculum coordinator and committees persists and is constantly being developed as new ideas and reports materialize. In this way, supervisors and teachers may participate in the process of curriculum development or, for other professional reasons, agree to use and edit curriculums designed by committees in which they did not participate. A principal does not have to be on the curriculum committee to be successful using the Big Four approach, especially if district size limits the number of committee participants. If the district does not have a centralized curriculum development process, then the task does have to be coordinated by the principal.

Similarly, the fourth component of the Big Four—revitalizing feedback methods specifically in grading and reporting—requires some district responsibility and the commitment to purchase and support an electronic record-keeping system for tracking benchmark scores or grades, generating internal reports and report cards for parents or guardians, and storing long-term data. A relational database provides the principal with ways to reorganize data in order to find patterns and make program changes. Centralized decisions about grading scales, homework policies, and frequency of reports can benefit building leaders in that the practice adds more viewpoints to decisions and lifts the burden of reinventing the wheel. Likewise, site-based decision making can work to resolve these problems.

In the next three chapters, we discuss how principals or coaches strategically improve learning by discussing the beginning, middle, and end of lessons with teachers. In each chapter, we address purposes for clinically addressing that segment of the lesson, important aspects of the lesson segment for teachers and supervisors, and examples of some learning approaches appropriate for various grade levels or subject areas. Some principals find the map of details of the Teaching Schema for Master Learners in Figure 2.7 useful when observing or conversing with a teacher. The strategies in this figure are discussed in the chapters to come.

FIGURE 2.7

A Strategy Map to the Teaching Schema for Master Learners

G: Goal Setting for the Learners: Benchmarks and Objectives

Read it	Predict it
Rewrite it	Connect it
Score it	

A: Access Prior Knowledge

Picture or object	Question or hypothesis
Story or analogy	Partner strategies
Summary or review	

N: Acquire New Information—Declarative, Procedural, or Both

To acquire declarative knowledge: Gather and organize
To acquire procedural knowledge: Follow steps and practice

A: Apply Knowledge—a Thinking Skill or Practice

To process declarative knowledge:

Knowledge	Recall (facts or method); Classify
Comprehension	Concept/convention formation; Predict (if, then)
Apply	Compare; Make an analogy
Analyze	Express a point of view; Identify a system or structure
Synthesize	Form and test a hypothesis; Solve a problem
Evaluate	Make a decision; Argue or persuade; Make a judgment or critique

To process procedural knowledge:
Shape and use in a new situation
Use self-regulating skills and character traits

G: Generalize or Summarize Knowledge Learned

Paper-and-pencil	Physical representations
Computer-assisted	Anecdotal examples
Partner strategies	

• **Homework** to extend the school day, as needed

• **Assessment tasks,** including quizzes, tests, or common assessments

In each case, the grade-level curriculum standard (benchmark) ties the conversation about the prepared lesson plan to the data collected by the supervisor during the observation. Supervisors will also find that they are more easily able to extend the conversation by comparing these classroom data to state test or common assessment scores in a meaningful way. Whether the dialogue occurs during planning, after observing a class, or both remains at the discretion of the supervisor, but the result is a guided conversation that improves student learning.

Supervisor Voice

Layne Parmenter, Early Childhood and Elementary School Principal

A former high school English teacher, Layne decided to become an early childhood and elementary principal because he believed that better learning in high school began with better learning in the primary grades. Making the transition gave him a new outlook on teaching and learning. As Layne discusses here, his experience as a principal has reinforced for him the value of feedback correlated with Schema implementation.

Scripting Left Me Unsure

I raced down the hall to Noelle's classroom. Caught up with resolving a playground issue, I had lost track of time and was now late for our scheduled observation. This wouldn't be just any observation, either. Noelle was using the Teaching Schema for Master Learners in her planning, and she had asked me to reference the same tool when observing her lesson. I had heard the Schema described in the teacher in-service workshop, but this would be my first time using it as a supervisor.

As I bustled in the door with laptop under my arm, I realized I was not sure where I had saved the document for the Schema on my laptop. Noelle and the students had already started the lesson. I flipped open an empty file and decided to wing it. I would find the template for the Schema later and then copy and paste my notes into it.

As I usually did for observations, I typed a running commentary of what was happening in the class. I tried to remember the pieces of the Schema

("Let's see: The steps in the Schema abbreviate to GANAG. The first *G* is for goal setting . . . "), but soon I was consumed with trying to keep up with transcribing Noelle's lesson. Worrying about the lesson sequence she was using faded pretty quickly from my mind.

I kept a detailed record of what happened in the lesson, but I summed it up much as I did all the other lessons I had observed: "pretty good." The youngsters were fairly attentive and seemed to be getting the gist of the lesson. After class, the children headed outside for recess and I stayed to talk with Noelle, thinking that she would bring up the Schema to guide our discussion.

Because I wasn't quite sure where to start, I told her I liked her use of the Smartboard. I stated that it was clear that she had designed the lesson to teach students the associative and commutative properties in math. But as I skimmed my notes, I realized that what I'd captured were all arbitrary details. I bogged down, Noelle didn't really say much, and I remembered why I *never* stay after a lesson to talk! I had thought that planning to the Teaching Schema for Master Learners was supposed to help teachers and supervisors discuss lessons afterward. So why wasn't it helping us?

Despite having performed observations quite a bit, I was suddenly unsure about what to say regarding the lesson. Partially, I feared saying the wrong thing—that my comments would make Noelle reluctant to follow any advice or instructions I gave her. As the students started to drift back in from recess, I excused myself and went down the hall, pretty dissatisfied with myself and with how the observation went. I didn't think I'd given Noelle feedback or information that she could use to improve her teaching, and I definitely knew I'd given her nothing that would improve student learning. I vowed to find the Teaching Schema for Master Learners template and go in next time with the GANAG steps all set up and ready to go.

A Whole New Way

The next teacher on my observation list, Lisa, had given me my share of problems in the past—something she herself is the first to admit! I knew Lisa didn't care for being observed. In fact, she had been known to patronize me during the post-observation conference and later question me mercilessly about instructional issues in front of the staff.

This time I had made sure that Lisa knew that I was using the Schema as a lens for examining her lesson. The template is simple; why did I think I needed to *find it* when I watched Noelle? I opened a blank document and typed the following letters:

G

A

N

A

G

I entered the class a few minutes early to watch the transition from the previous activity. Lisa began by clarifying the goal for the lesson and tying it to a benchmark related to different kinds of money and making change. The goal was set. I typed in a few notes after the first *G*. She then engaged the students by having them restate the goal in their own words to each other.

Next, Lisa introduced the idea of different bills, like a $10 bill and a $2 bill. The students took part effortlessly, adding comments about different kinds of money they had seen or used. I noted this discussion as the "access prior knowledge" cue—the first *A* in GANAG. For the next 20 minutes, Lisa role-played with students how to make change and continued with new information and application. Meanwhile, I effortlessly added observation notes to the GANAG organizer.

When we met to discuss the observation later in the day, I realized that at no time during the lesson had I had a moment's hesitation about what I was looking for. That was a first for me! Lisa and I analyzed the lesson, Schema step by Schema step. We agreed that she had set the goal for the lesson, and we discussed her use of cues to access students' experiences with money and focus them for the lesson. During our meeting, it occurred to me that the conference lacked any feeling of judgment or finger-pointing. We were merely looking at the lesson together through the lens of GANAG.

The conference ended with a plan for Lisa to work on giving her students a chance to generalize at the end of the lesson (the final *G* in GANAG). She had felt that lack of time meant it was better to do the generalization the next day; I gave her my perspective, which was that it's better to let students sum up their new learning immediately rather than wait. The conference was an excellent, productive discussion. I had more confidence that the feedback I was giving her would have some impact. Lisa appeared to be gaining something from our discussion as well.

I returned to my office, sat down, and thought, "Wow! What a difference that made." I was already looking forward to my next observation.

Focusing on the Lesson, Not the Teacher

Each time I use the Teaching Schema for Master Learners to guide my lesson observations, I become more and more enthusiastic about it. First, it focuses me on the core elements of the lesson, based on student learning, and gives me just a few items to watch for. Second, it gives the teachers and me an external focus for the post-observation debriefing. I can ask teachers how they thought they did on any or all of the GANAG components, and suddenly we're discussing the lesson, not the teacher.

As an evaluator, I've always felt I was being too critical if I needed to say less-than-positive things, even though I meant well and sincerely wanted the teacher to improve his or her teaching performance. It always felt like I was criticizing the person, not the lesson. I never really knew how to get around that until I started using the Schema in my supervision practices.

Another teacher and I had a very enthusiastic discussion of a lesson on place values for her 2nd grade class. Zoe had done something I'd not seen before: in the last step of the lesson, where the children generalize what they've learned, she let every student in her class have an opportunity to respond. After the lesson, she came into the conference room smiling and said, "So is the generalization step in GANAG for the students or for the teacher?" The question stopped me for a minute, because up to that point, I'd always seen it as being for the students—a way to close out the lesson, like a bookend, or provide closure for the neurons firing around in the their heads. I thought for a minute and said, "I think it's both." She grinned at me. It was the first time *that's* ever happened in a post-observation conference!

Zoe and I went on to have an enthusiastic discussion about the merits of generalizing for both parties. We noted that the students certainly get a chance to summarize their learning, but the teacher, particularly in this case, gets to assess what the students know. Zoe figured that about 30 percent of her class had really completely understood the concept, but she assured me she would persevere until they all got it. We continued talking intently, reluctant to end our conversation even when other teachers entered the room for a meeting.

One "Improved" Principal

I find that some teachers really tend to excel at one of the GANAG components. Zoe's last step, for example, was unique. Shortly after I'd seen it, I watched Gwen teach a sight word to her 1st graders and learned about teaching the step of applying new information (the N in GANAG). She was teaching them the word *what* using a multitude of techniques that included writing the word on the board, having students "write" the letters on a partner's back, having them read a series of sentences using the word to a partner, and finally having them write short sentences incorporating the word. The students used *what* in such a variety of ways and contexts that it would be nearly impossible for them not to learn it well.

I've also begun to see lessons in a new way in a very short time. In a lesson on sentence variety in a 4th grade class, the students were assigned to come up to the board and tell which group a predicate modifier would fit in: *where, why, when,* or *how*. The students performed flawlessly time and again. It occurred to me that they really didn't need any more practice; they had mastered the procedural knowledge, as discussed in the Schema's goal-setting step. I brought this observation up in the conference with the teacher, and the teacher made appropriate adjustments.

I have begun to realize just how often teachers are teaching information students already know. I assume they do this in an effort to look competent and proficient, but before I used the Teaching Schema for Master Learners, I never noticed it. Since using the Schema, I do notice. More than that, I am now able to empathize with teachers over the fact that students consistently need new knowledge . . . and to ask them kindly to teach some new information to the students while I am there to observe it.

Another thing I noticed was that in the first round of observations using the Schema, very few teachers actually did all five steps, even knowing I was coming to watch them and was targeting the Schema particularly. Most did one or several steps brilliantly but left one out—usually the generalization at the end. Afterward, when I pointed out the omission, they all said something along the lines of, "Well, I just ran out of time," as if that somehow made it all OK.

I think the hardest step to do well is accessing prior knowledge. Most of what I tend to see for this step is a review of the lesson from the day before. While that is sound enough, it's kind of a low-budget way to access prior knowledge. I'm now encouraging teachers to look for more creative, enticing ways of doing the same thing and at the very least *vary* the way they perform this step. We talk about ways to do that in our staff meetings, I share what I've seen in lessons, and I ask teachers to pitch in with strategies they've used. It is a process of learning for all of us, and we're making progress. For evidence, I just think back to my conversation with Lisa from several weeks ago, in which she thanked me for the feedback after I observed her class. Another first!

I may be a regular guy from Wyoming, but I just might be that *one principal at a time.*

3

The Beginning of the Lesson

After reading this chapter, you should be able to

• Explain why teachers should share grade-level standards with students at the beginning of a lesson.

• Recommend a variety of lesson-beginning techniques teachers can use to stimulate learning.

• Advise teachers on ways to create measurable grade-level standards.

THERE ARE LOTS OF WAYS TO BEGIN A LESSON. DWIGHT MOTT, A HIGH SCHOOL principal, offers a few ways to categorize them:

• Homework review
• DOL/DOG (daily oral language/geography)
• Day starter
• Socializing, but appearing appropriate

These are familiar to most of us, and you can probably think of a few more types of lesson-openers, depending on the grade levels or subjects that you have taught or observed over the years. Still, many of us remember Madeline Hunter's admonishment that teachers need to "take advantage of the learning propulsion inherent in the beginning of our class and not waste that beginning 'prime time' on 'soap opera activities'" (1982, p. 27). In other words, we believe all good lesson-openers are purposeful ones.

Purposeful lesson beginnings should produce evidence that students have been made aware of what they will know or do better by the end of the designated class period. Lesson beginnings should also access prior student knowledge to support successful learning. Supervisors can determine the extent to which teachers foster student awareness and readiness by looking for two separate components of the Teaching Schema for Master Learners: *G: Set the GOAL* and *A: ACCESS prior student knowledge.*

Guidance on Goal Setting

Stating, showing, or reviewing curriculum targets at the beginning of a lesson is nonnegotiable. In *Classroom Instruction That Works* (2001), Marzano, Pickering, and Pollock identify setting objectives and giving students feedback on progress toward those objectives as one of the most important strategies a teacher can use. At the beginning of the lesson, an observing principal wants to see indications that all students clearly understand that lesson's objectives.

Observing principals should be aware that the lesson grade-level curriculum standards expressed at the beginning of a class are often a continuation or extension of what students learned or practiced in the previous lesson, and that teaching students to gain proficiency on these goals might require additional instruction beyond the current class session. However, the curricular statements should explicitly direct student performance, assessment, and enrichment. Barbara Herzog, an assistant superintendent who supervises principals, tells us that in her experience, "Showing a teacher the important difference between *stating a measurable or scoreable learning goal for the students* versus *stating directions for an activity* may be the most important contribution that a principal can communicate with a teacher to impact learning."

As the lesson progresses, the principal should see the teacher structuring instruction so that students receive feedback in various ways to ensure each is aware of his or her progress. Lessons that are structured around clearly written curriculum targets and include meaningful and ongoing feedback to students give them opportunities to learn new information, practice learned knowledge, and apply their knowledge to generate original ideas and develop new skills.

In the discussion that follows, we use the terms *grade-level curriculum standards* and *benchmarks* synonymously: both indicate the aims of the lesson.

Because many schools use synonyms of these terms to indicate the stated learning goal, in the section "Modifying or Unpacking Benchmarks," beginning on page 67, we explain some technical differences that may be useful to a principal when offering teachers feedback about unpacking or editing district or state standards to make the targets measurable.

Why Sharing Benchmarks Is Essential

The consensus about goal setting suggests that a person who sets a goal and maps out a realistic course for achieving it is more likely to work conscientiously toward it than a person who proceeds without such planning. Transferring that idea to the classroom, the student who knows a lesson's benchmarks and objectives is more likely to regulate his or her behaviors to make progress toward those ends.

Within the first one to three minutes of a class, an observing principal should see that the teacher is (1) identifying appropriate curriculum benchmarks (and objectives) for a lesson and (2) employing a technique that lets students assess themselves and become aware of what they are going to learn, or learn to do better, in that lesson.

One principal we worked with described observing a science class without having first conducted a pre-observation conference with the teacher. She entered the classroom and saw this lesson goal written on the board: "Create a model of the atom." (The principal admitted that when she read the statement, she immediately wondered *how* the students would go about creating that model.) The class began with the teacher commenting briefly that the common representation of the atom—a nucleus corralled by two elliptical diagrams, with small, solid-looking circles indicating the presence of electrons—was an inaccurate depiction. The majority of the lesson consisted of the students copying bullet-pointed notes from the teacher's fact-filled PowerPoint presentation. It ended, somewhat frenetically, with the teacher calling out a reading assignment for homework, a date for the next test, and a reminder to bring materials for the school's recycling campaign. As students exited the classroom, the principal stopped a few and asked them about the lesson goal. Did they create a model of an atom, as the objective stated they would? They nonchalantly replied that they did not *think* that they had created a model of an atom but that they weren't really sure.

Contrast this scenario with what elementary school principal Janna Cochrane observed in 5th grade teacher Amy Ashton's class at the beginning of a math lesson on surface area. Amy clarified the conceptual benchmark and specific content objectives as follows:

> *Benchmark:* Students will understand and apply surface area concepts:
> • Know area formulas (circle, square, rectangle).
> • Know steps to find surface area.
> • Find surface area for various objects.
> • Predict uses for finding surface area.

With this information listed on the board, Amy proceeded to ask her students to self-assess their knowledge of the topics by giving her a "show of fingers" (one finger to indicate a little knowledge, four fingers to indicate lots of knowledge). She randomly questioned a few students, asking them to share what they knew about surface area. This informal feedback activity not only allowed Amy to unobtrusively assess the accuracy of student self-assessments but also helped the students focus on the lesson goal and check their own understanding. Throughout that lesson and subsequent lessons pertaining to the topic, Amy continued to ask students to score themselves (informally again) in response to instruction. There were also other tasks—such as quizzes and assignments—for which students received more formal grades or scores linked to the curriculum benchmarks. Amy recorded these scores in her grade book, and the students kept a record of them as well in their own math notebooks.

Janna Cochrane, Amy's principal, believes that the power of feedback to influence the learner provides a salient reason for setting measurable goals at the onset of a lesson. The literature supports this point of view. In a review of research on feedback, Hattie and Timperley (2007) state that "the main purpose of feedback is to reduce discrepancies between current understandings and performance and the goal" (p. 86). Who better to provide effective feedback about progress toward curriculum goals than the teacher—someone who is expert enough to teach and organize instruction so students can learn from each other and detect the errors in their own learning? Setting the aim at the beginning of the lesson and ensuring that students clearly understand the objective creates an anchor to which students and teachers can refer to make feedback that much more meaningful; it assists students in assessing their own progress and working to reduce discrepancies between what they know and what they can know in relation to curriculum goals.

Both pre- and post-observation conferences and careful observation during the goal-setting segment of a lesson can further support collaborative planning and reflection that are specifically targeted to establishing goals and introducing them to students. During conferences, the observing principal can provide feedback to the teacher regarding (1) the robust nature of the benchmarks and objectives and (2) the ways in which the different strategies used to share the benchmarks and objectives can initiate and invigorate learning.

Supervisor Summary

Students should grasp the goal of each lesson within the first few minutes of class.

- ○ Devote time during the pre-observation conference to discussing the lesson's goal or goals with the teacher.
- ○ Note ways in which the teacher clearly conveys the goal or goals at the outset of the lesson, and look for evidence that students understand which knowledge or skills they will need to demonstrate in order to verify their achievement of the goal.
- ○ Remind teachers that a discussion of the activities that will occur during the lesson is only viable if a relationship is drawn between planned activities and measurable student progress toward the goal or goals.

Strategies for Varying Lesson Openings

Gaining students' attention by setting goals works only until the brain's need for novelty leads them to be distracted by some other interference. The supervisor's challenge is to recommend ways that the teacher can alternate class-opening tactics in a way that engages students' needs for novelty and still upholds the importance of goal setting.

Elementary school principal Sara Austin told us that most of the teachers she observes write the benchmarks on the board and say them aloud at the onset of a lesson. As she observes classes, she often wonders how effective this approach is, and she asked us to suggest additional ways that a teacher could present benchmarks and objectives to stimulate student interest and support understanding without unnecessarily complicating the beginning of the lesson.

We came up with five categories of strategies supervisors might recommend to their teachers, purposefully choosing ones that most teachers already know: *Read it, Rewrite it, Score it, Predict it,* and *Connect it.* Our experience confirms what many teachers disclose about their practice: that they are "in a pedagogical automaticity rut," defaulting to a single, familiar way of starting the class. Although they do know other strategies to use at the beginning of a lesson, they welcome uncomplicated reminders about different tactics that will help them be more effective. Let's take a closer look at each of these approaches.

"Read it" strategies. For many teachers and students, posting lesson goals on a daily basis reduces confusion and creates a habit of expecting to address the goals. In this approach, teachers read, verbally state, or have students read the posted lesson goal aloud. Supervisors might suggest teachers consider the various ways to present the written goals, including on a whiteboard, Smartboard, transparency, wiki or blog, in a unit packet, or in the interactive notebook. Because benchmarks and objectives often contain academic vocabulary needed to make the lesson meaningful, teacher Jenny Thomes reminds us that English language learners (ELLs) need to hear the words spoken as they read them; this extra step also allows ELLs another opportunity to ask about the words.

"Rewrite it" strategies. Here, students rewrite or represent each goal in their own words, as they understand it. Supervisors might remind teachers that this approach is a good way to help students personalize benchmarks and objectives. When science teacher Julie Goodelle teaches genetics, for example, she provides students with a lesson benchmark and objectives to guide learning about traits of organisms, some of which are inherited and others that result from the organism's interactions with the environment. Julie instructs her 9th graders to rewrite the statements in a way that makes them more personal and supports their own understanding. For the original benchmark "Knows that a typical cell of any organism may contain specific genetic traits that may be modified by environmental influences," a student might write, "I would like to understand whether or not cystic fibrosis is an inherited trait or a result of inter-action with the environment, because my neighbor was diagnosed with CF."

A principal might also recommend that the teacher use pictures or other nonlinguistic models to show a different representation of the benchmarks and provoke interest in the content or the procedures, or ask students to "rewrite" the benchmarks in picture form.

Students can also learn to generate goals for themselves. For example, a teacher might ask students to elaborate on the stated objective by creating a new goal that aligns with the curriculum. In a Family Consumer Science class, for example, the content benchmark might read, "Understands space needs based on a client's specifications." A student might rephrase the goals as follows: "I'm going to survey five or more people who own businesses to find out what kind of space they would like and what kind they can afford."

"Score it" strategies. With this approach, teachers encourage students to self-evaluate the understanding they already have of the goal. When faced with performance criteria or knowledge to be measured relative to curriculum benchmarks and objectives, teachers prompt learners to ask themselves, "What degree of skill or knowledge do I already possess that will help me carry out this procedure or demonstrate achievement of this objective?" By evaluating their understanding, students prepare to improve their skill and knowledge.

Principals can suggest that teachers facilitate self-scoring or self-evaluation by setting up a matrix of benchmarks and objectives on which students can record their scores and chart their progress on a day-to-day basis. The matrix might be on paper or created as an electronic file. High school history teacher Gail Goff uses this method to coach students to focus on daily objectives (short-term goals) and on benchmarks (long-term goals) over a series of days (see Figure 3.1).

According to kindergarten teacher Anne Hughes and 2nd grade teacher Gillian Reeves, self-evaluation is important for younger students because it allows them to verbalize their assessment, which adds to their confidence lev-els. A principal might encourage teachers in the primary grades to prompt students to represent how well they understand a benchmark physically rather than verbally: perhaps "Give me a thumbs up, thumbs down, or thumbs to the side" or, "Show me one, two, three, or four fingers." Scoring themselves in a

---

FIGURE 3.1

Student Self-Assessment Matrix

Use this chart to determine how well you understand what you need to know to be successful in this unit. If you do not know this material, it is your responsibility to read the text over again, see me for help, or go to the help lab!

Rate your understanding: 4 = Outstanding; 3 = Competent; 2 = Needs Improvement; 1 = Poor

I. The Stage Is Set
You understand the role of nationalism in conflicts within different nations such as the Ottoman & Austro-Hungarian Empires.

4	3	2	1

II. The Guns of August
You understand the extent to which militarism, alliances, imperialism, and nationalism contributed to World War I. You understand the strategies of the Allied and Central Powers, including the Schlieffen Plan.

4	3	2	1

III. A New Kind of Conflict
You understand how the scientific and technological changes of the early 20th century impacted the war. You understand whether the "technology" and strategies contributed to a stalemate.

4	3	2	1

IV. Winning the War
You understand the impact of the war on the Ottoman Empire (e.g., the Armenian Massacre). You understand the power of propaganda in influencing people.

4	3	2	1

Source: Gail Goff, Baker High School, Baldwinsville, New York.

---

swift, criterion-based opener helps students connect to the lesson topic, and this personal assessment adds an element of tension that can engage an otherwise unconnected learner.

"Predict it" strategies. Here, teachers present "teasers" generated from the previous lesson that offer clues to the lesson goal. Instead of starting class with a tired review question ("Does anyone remember what we did yesterday?"), a teacher might simply state the benchmarks and objectives from the previous day as a prompt for introducing new ones or might seek out an unexpected way of stimulating student thinking. For example, if Amy Ashton's 5th graders are working on the benchmark for understanding surface area, she might start the second day by showing an object such as a cylindrical oatmeal package, and then ask students to think about what they focused on yesterday and predict the learning goals of the upcoming lesson. If the day before they learned about the surface area of cubes or spheres, they might guess that the natural next step would be to find surface area for more complex objects. Similarly, many teachers combine tasks by asking students to use the summary from the end of the previous lesson to predict or brainstorm where they may be headed.

"Connect it" strategies. These strategies involve teachers connecting student effort to the lesson goal. A critical connection that the supervisor can suggest to help students learn better is to address effort as a lesson objective. Many students do not believe that effort improves performance, and often the teacher's accurate evaluation of a student's effort occurs only after the fact. When Bess Scott was the principal of Goodrich Middle School, some graduate students partnered with her staff to develop the Goodrich Task Effort Rubric, shown in Figure 3.2, as a means of increasing student effort. (Goodrich Middle's School's motto: "We work hard. We get smart. We work harder. We get smarter!") Teachers there have since become accustomed to asking students to evaluate their effort levels at the beginning of class as a way to affirm how they think they might attempt to learn each day's benchmarks; at the end of the lesson, they can reflect on how their effort affected their performance.

Goals for Students, Not Teachers

The beginning of a lesson is critical for awakening the learner to the purpose of the lesson and also for establishing assessment criteria. Many principals tell us that in their districts or schools, all teachers know that curriculum benchmarks must be observable to the students. However, when we enter classrooms, more often than not we note that the teachers do this solely by dedicating a section on the board to the daily agenda: a list of three or four activities. It's true that for many teachers and students, simply posting lesson goals on a daily basis helps reduce confusion, provides a basis for addressing goals, and creates a habit of expecting to address the goals. And when we ask

FIGURE 3.2
Goodrich Middle School Task Effort Rubric

Goodrich Effort

- I worked on the task until it was complete.
- I pushed myself to continue working even when the task seemed difficult/easy.
- I used the difficulties of the task as opportunities to learn and understand.
- I used the ease of the task to celebrate what I have learned.

Satisfactory Effort

- I worked on the task until it was complete.
- I continued working when the task seemed difficult/easy.
- I used the task as an opportunity to learn and understand.

Inconsistent Effort

- I used some effort in completing the task.
- I stopped working when the task seemed difficult/easy.

Minimal Effort

- I used very little effort to complete the task.

No Effort

- I made no attempt to complete the task.

Source: Bess Scott and the staff of Goodrich Middle School, Lincoln, Nebraska.

teachers about their daily benchmarks or objectives, they generally point to these kinds of agendas.

Because curriculum development and supervision evolved by emphasizing teacher goals, teachers learned to habitually "check themselves" as they planned activities to ensure each lesson covered all the district's requisite curriculum targets. Using the Schema suggests a more student-centered reason for setting the goals. The curriculum documents should clearly distinguish between *activities students might perform in a class period* and *the curriculum benchmarks that serve as criteria for measurement*. The pre-observation dialogue between a principal and a teacher should include this clarification.

Supervisor Summary

During the first few minutes of a lesson, the teacher should employ techniques that engage students when introducing the lesson goal. Techniques should vary from lesson to lesson.

○ Use pre-observation conferences to recommend different techniques a teacher can use to introduce goals, including "Read it," "Rewrite it," "Score it," "Predict it," and "Connect it" strategies.

○ Explain that you'll be looking for at least one of these techniques to be incorporated into the beginning of a lesson.

Modifying or "Unpacking" Benchmarks

In Chapter 2, we stated that the curriculum development process could be centralized. This implies that a teacher would use a district-developed curriculum document to access "just-right" grade-level benchmarks and objectives derived from documents of state or national standards. In many cases, however, districts adopt state standards and benchmarks, advising teachers to use them because the state test items align to those documents. For a complete discourse on the usefulness of state documents, we encourage you to read reports such as the Fordham Foundation's *State of the State Standards* (Finn, Julian, & Petrelli, 2006).

Briefly, a standard that appears in state documents, for example, is intended to span the K–12 curriculum. Most national documents show grade-cluster or grade-level statements (benchmarks) for each of the standards to show classroom teachers where they might incorporate age-appropriate knowl-edge and skills into their lessons. With good examples available online (such as the documents produced by departments of education in states like California, Massachusetts, and Indiana), principals can guide teachers to "unpack" the state benchmarks to produce a measurable group of epigrammatic, grade-level-appropriate statements that lend themselves to scoring on a daily or every-other-day basis. A bank of specific content for all of the grade-level benchmarks may also be useful to teachers.

Chapter 2 of *Improving Student Learning One Teacher at a Time* (Pollock, 2007) details how to unpack state standards to create classroom-ready bench-marks. These benchmarks follow the Goldilocks rule: not too broad, not too specific, but *just right*. A helpful metaphor is to think of the standard as a manila folder, containing a variety of organized facts and procedures. The description you'd write on the tab on that folder—the succinct way of describing its con-tents—would be the "just-right benchmark."

Another critical need regarding the curriculum content standards and their preparation for implementation is determining whether they address declarative knowledge or procedural knowledge, or whether they are self-regulation skills or character traits. Because this determination ties so directly to the teacher's decision about which instructional strategy to apply, we will save that discus-sion for the next chapter, in which we discuss the middle of the lesson.

Supervisor Summary

Lesson goals should align with district curriculum.

○ Familiarize yourself with national and international reports such as the Fordham Foundation's *State of the State Standards*.

○ Call teachers' attention to state and national standards and how to use them to create measurable, "just-right" learning targets for daily lessons.

In the next section, we discuss the other component of the beginning of a lesson that principals can focus on as a way to help teachers improve instruction.

General Guidelines for Accessing Prior Student Knowledge

Kirk Delwiche, principal of Weyauwega and Fremont Elementary Schools, contributed this to our "One Principal at a Time" blog (www.improvestudent learning.com):

> It is amazing to watch effective teachers pull and tug the strings of linkage within students' memories to activate prior knowledge, but I have a question. What are some ways to help teachers vary the strategies or arouse the excitement level of the students during this segment of the Teaching Schema for Master Learners?

Principal Erin Kohl described for us a probability lesson for 3rd graders. As planned, the lesson would begin with the teacher flipping a coin and then progress toward formulating conclusions and predicting outcomes based on data, as stated in the math benchmark about probability.

To access prior student knowledge, the teacher asked her students if they had ever flipped a coin and called "heads" or "tails" to make a decision. The 3rd graders responded, as they do to questions such as these, with enthusiasm expressed by scooting themselves to the edges of their seats, waving their hands in the air, and fairly bursting to speak. After describing the strict rules for flipping a coin, the teacher permitted students to share personal narratives, technical descriptions, and one very detailed account of the formulaic tactic used in a national sports venue. Twelve minutes passed. Students were definitely engaged. But, Erin pointed out, sometime during those 12 minutes the measurable objective of the lesson was lost. Students were supposed to be thinking about probability, predicting, and drawing conclusions. It seems to her they had been sidetracked with stories about flipping coins.

This vignette highlights two issues. First, the "accessing prior student knowledge" activity (the first *A* in GANAG) should last only two or three minutes—just enough time to spike students' interest. Second, a lesson can easily stray from its objective if teachers aren't careful. Certainly we have all experienced this type of lesson beginning, when an activity meant to be the precursor to the pursuit of an objective becomes the objective itself.

Interestingly, teachers often tell us that they do not deliberately plan the prompt to access prior knowledge; instead, they might perform extemporaneously or use a prompt from a book without necessarily considering how the students' responses will affect the rest of the lesson. First grade teacher Dana Zigler admits that for years she cued student learning at the onset of the lesson because she thought she was supposed to do *something,* but she never spent much time considering how this process was actually helping students "mine" their existing knowledge and connect it to the new information in the lesson. Now that she does realize the importance of accessing prior knowledge, she finds it the most difficult part of the lesson to prepare, noting that coming up with appropriate, effective cues and examples requires a teacher to be an expert in both the content area and the students' age-group-related interests and development levels.

From J. F. Herbart in the 1800s to Madeline Hunter in the 1970s to Donna Ogle in the 1990s, messages about engaging a learner at the beginning of the lesson have taken a dramatic turn. Herbart recommended a highly teacher-directed opening for presenting to students what they should know but did not place any importance on eliciting students' thinking (Gutek, 1991). The Hunter model (1982) recommends that the teacher engage the students through an anticipatory set. Donna Ogle (1986) recommends stretching the learner more, citing neurological research that indicates that the learner who responds to a prompt or stimulus with previous knowledge will more likely clarify misunderstanding and connect the new information more efficiently.

William Christen and Thomas Murphy (1991) synthesized research about increasing comprehension by activating prior knowledge and came to this conclusion:

> The learning environment needs to provide a setting that incorporates stability and familiarity. It should be able to satisfy the mind's enormous curiosity and hunger for discovery, challenge, and novelty. Creating an opportunity to challenge our students to call on their collective experiences (prior knowledge) is essential. Through this process we move students from memorizing information to meaningful learning and begin the journey of connecting learning events rather than remembering bits and pieces. Prior knowledge is an essential element in this quest for making meaning. (p. 2)

Researchers agree that activating prior knowledge can increase comprehension. Teachers can use simple strategies such as brainstorming or posing a situation to prompt prior knowledge in order to build new concepts and principles, details and characteristics, and associations or similar experiences.

Supervisor Summary

For two to three minutes at the beginning of the lesson, before or after setting the goal, the teacher should access prior knowledge from individual students or from the collective experiences of the class.

○ Ensure that class activities designed to engage students are actually allowing the teacher to access prior student knowledge and are not an end in themselves.

○ Plan the prompt purposefully to cue learners to call upon their personal knowledge.

Strategies for Accessing Prior Knowledge

Many teachers tell us that the biggest hurdle is retraining themselves to deliberately plan to access prior knowledge for every lesson. However, to answer Kirk's question from the beginning of the section, there are several general ways teachers can facilitate this process. Some of the best bets are to use research-based strategies that Jane and her colleagues found in the research examples (Marzano et al., 2001), including *picture or object, story or analogy, summary or review, question or hypothesis,* and *partner-based* strategies.

Picture or object strategies. Using a nonlinguistic picture or object in a classroom usually attracts students' curiosity. When Jackie Campbell's 3rd graders came to class one day, they noticed three new potted plants on the teacher's workbench, but one of the plants drooped so badly that the stem hung down almost touching the leg of the table. It took only a minute for a curious 9-year-old to ask, "What is wrong with that plant? The other ones look fine."

Jackie purposefully plans her beginnings to capture that moment of "curiosity and hunger for discovery," even if it is mundane or plain. The students in her class could not help themselves—they were engaged in the quest to improve the health of the poor, sick plant.

Story or analogy strategies. We tend to love the oral tradition of storytelling, so it is a culturally comfortable way to begin a lesson. David Seabast began a high school class in a meditative manner by recounting the summer after his 7th grade year, when he mowed lawns to earn money to buy a BB gun. This story led directly to the basic tenets of economics: supply and demand, bartering, and different markets. His 9th graders easily engaged in the conversation because they, too, had earned money to negotiate with parents to buy electronic equipment, clothing, or tickets to events.

David smiles as he talks about how his planning and delivery changed once he felt allowed to "tell stories" to high school students. He admitted that he worried it did not appear as academic as starting by defining economic terms, but the results, he states, were dramatically positive for the learners.

Summary or review strategies. A seemingly spontaneous review of a previous lesson or assignment can certainly work to fire neurons. High school administrator Julie Mosher remarks that she often sees teachers ask students to summarize or review material from previous lectures. For example, the teacher might begin with a brainstorming technique that prompts the students to look through previous notes or labs in order to contribute to the class review.

Because brainstorming can stimulate so many ideas quickly, teachers can employ tactics to vary or focus tasks. Julie might suggest that an art teacher ask students to find 10 key terms in notes from the previous lesson in which they discussed techniques that applied to their ceramics project. The students can then share with a partner to reduce the list to five critical terms. Then, pairs of partners can share their lists, reducing them to three terms that can serve as a summary or review of the previous lesson. Such a conversation, reinforced by suggesting a number of terms to search, forces both extending knowledge and restricting it; therefore, the process motivates the learner to think more deeply about the topic.

Question or hypothesis strategies. Engaging a learner by asking a question or hypothesizing with "if/then" statements offers different opportunities to extend learning. When Scott Norton teaches landscaping, he asks students to consider what would happen to the growth of certain plant arrangements if the weather changed dramatically during a season. Similarly Ann Hughes, a primary teacher, asks students to generate if/then statements about the social studies topic of reading maps. For example: "*If* the map has color, *then* we can tell whether there is water or land." This activity leads students to review the characteristics about maps they learned in a previous lesson in order to consider new knowledge about using maps.

Partner-based strategies. David Johnson and Roger Johnson, who wrote extensively about cooperative learning (1999), often remarked that two heads really are better than one. This is particularly true for accessing prior knowledge in classes with great student diversity. Sharon Pernisi, a teacher at Huntington K–8 School, describes the positive effect of applying the partner factor to any of the aforementioned prompts, especially in her math classes. She indicates that peers can frequently provide clarifying prompts, as they are often aware of each other's misconceptions. Partners can restate or interpret the prompt in ways that engage other learners more deeply.

Each of the previous categories of strategies is discussed in *Classroom Instruction That Works* (Marzano et al., 2001), and each represents strategies that principals should recommend to teachers to help students retain information. When the lesson begins with a deliberate exercise to access prior student knowledge, the remainder of the lesson is more likely to be focused toward a goal, because the students connect what they already know to what they will learn about new facts, concepts, principles, or procedures.

Supervisor Summary

Teachers should vary the methods they use to access prior student knowledge from lesson to lesson.

○ Remind teachers that the process of accessing prior student knowledge can include activities such as brainstorming, considering real-life situations from which students can extrapolate prior knowledge, or other research-based strategies.

Principals can help teachers realize that regardless of the length of the class, students still need the first few minutes at the beginning of the lesson to find their cognitive bearings. Beginning a lesson by setting the curriculum benchmark and then cuing previous knowledge is a way for teachers to display academic courtesy to the students. The students will be more likely to engage and later retain the knowledge. Similarly, in the upcoming chapter about the end of a lesson, we stress that principals should take note of how teachers ask students to summarize what they understand as a result of the lesson. We call these times at the beginning and end of lessons the "bookends"—the G at the beginning and the G at the end of GANAG in the Teaching Schema for Master Learners.

Supervisor Voice

Janna Cochrane, Elementary School Principal

Janna had a challenge on her hands. Students with disabilities at her school were not meeting adequate yearly progress goals, and that had to change. For a year, Janna and Jane worked together with the staff, meeting once a month to focus on the Big Four and implementing the Teaching Schema for Master Learners. Their efforts paid off— in terms of improved (and more collaborative) teaching and improved learning.

A Staff on a Quest

You know something good is happening when a 3rd grader stops you in the hallway and says, "We had a really great lesson today, Mrs. Cochrane! Our teacher GANAG-ed reading class, and we all learned a lot better."

Studying the Big Four approach started a cultural revolution of sorts here at Carl Traeger Elementary School in Wisconsin. We were drawn to *Improving Student Learning One Teacher at a Time* (Pollock, 2007) because of the emphasis it places on providing students with feedback keyed to quality learning targets. Our school population includes a large number of special education students, primarily with disabilities in the areas of speech and language, specific learning disabilities, emotional behavior disabilities, and autism. As a staff, we were on a quest to raise achievement across the board and close the achievement gap between our students with disabilities and their general education peers. This quest led us to the Big Four and the Teaching Schema for Master Learners.

Benefits for All

What we call "the phenomenon" began with our regular education teachers. They learned to score to benchmarks and plan lessons using proven instructional strategies to increase student achievement. Everything centered on the idea of feedback, and a shift in practice began to occur. The common vocabulary introduced by the Schema (chiefly the GANAG steps) was a connecting element among the staff. GANAG became a verb in our culture: teachers would frequently remark "We need to GANAG that" with regard to our own professional development and collaboration. This change to a standards-based approach produced classroom data and test scores that proved our efforts were having an impact in the classroom; we were truly changing student learning.

A parallel shift took place in special education. As we entered the world of the Big Four and the Schema, we were unsure about how we would adapt the approach for special education students or what impact it would have on them. We knew that some of the management strategies we used, such as visual and sensory input, could benefit all students, and we saw very quickly that planning lessons to the GANAG components benefited special education students in ways we had not imagined. Reciprocal learning about the method between our regular education teachers and our special education teachers opened up new doors for collaboration and communication.

In the past, when our special education teachers collected lesson plans from their regular education colleagues, there had been some difficulty because every teacher recorded lessons differently. With all of the lessons written in the Schema's GANAG format, special education teachers were armed with everything they needed to reinforce instruction and provide the necessary accommodations for special education students. A consistency emerged that allowed special education teachers to focus on assisting their students in attaining the learning goals rather than wasting valuable time identifying the goal in the actual lesson or probing for greater understanding with the regular education teacher. Collaboration time and conversation could be centered on the student and learning rather than on clarifying lesson plans.

Using GANAG to Support Goal Achievement and Knowledge Gains

Establishing the goal of the lesson not only provided greater clarity to all students but also allowed our special education staff to hone in on the truly vital elements of a lesson. They could make the appropriate accommodations for student learning without watering down the benchmark or expectations. The students also had a heightened awareness about what they were to focus on; for special education students who struggle with communication, this was valuable.

Accessing prior knowledge fires the neurons in the brain, allowing students to connect something they are familiar with to the upcoming learning. In the case of special education students, this is particularly critical, as many of them can make these connections only with prompting. Activities that cue students to share prior knowledge give staff the insight they need to help students connect what they already know and the new information the lesson will present.

Generalizing the learning at the end of a lesson benefits all children. Not only does it lock in their learning, but it is also a wonderful way to assess what they know and to inform future lesson planning. This benefit was amplified for our special education population. Overall, it is very difficult for students with disabilities to generalize their learning. Using GANAG, the staff generated alternative ways for these students to show what they had learned and provided extra time for them to process the learning. We came to believe that for many of our special education students, the learning that had just taken place would be lost without the generalization. Although generalizing information is often a laborious process for special needs students, it creates meaning for them. The success gained in truly learning the material has shown us again that while generalizing may be good for all students, it is vital to the success of our students with disabilities.

We have found that our special education students frequently need a quieter environment to apply their learning. The actual lesson may be interrupted by the need for a sensory break. Attention spans may not allow some students to tune in for all of the application of new information. Such situations brought us to the realization that once a child was removed from a lesson for reinforce-ment or additional instruction in a resource room, we needed to start GANAG all over again. The goal needed to be stated again so the child could recall the focus of the learning; staff needed to access prior knowledge again to help the child reconnect with the material; and so on. One teacher shared how she real-ized that by re-creating that connection in the resource room, the child had an additional opportunity to make a connection. It is quite common for special education students to need this additional connection. Once we were aware of this need, our interventions became much more effective.

Individualizing Schema Use

Individualization is essential in the Teaching Schema for Master Learners. Although the goal for our special education students usually stays the same, an individual plan for a special education student might state that the student needs a different way to access prior knowledge, apply the learning, or gener-alize. Not every student achieves the same goal in the same way. This sounds simple enough, but the consistency of using GANAG to plan lessons seemed to make the task of individualizing for a number of students easier.

Our students now ask for the elements of the Schema by name. They will ask teachers, "How will we access prior knowledge today?" Students have reminded their teacher to generalize with an exit ticket at the end of a math lesson. The language has become pervasive in our school—evidence of a true cultural change.

Now We All GANAG . . . and Have Reason to Brag

I cannot conclude without boasting a bit about our students' scores on the Wisconsin state assessments. Briefly, when we ran calculations on our state test scores, we found that in the first year, the gap between students with disabili-ties and their nondisabled peers decreased an average of 10 percent across the board. Here at Carl Traeger Elementary School, our work is not finished, but we know we are getting better as a staff—and we know our students are improving because of our efforts.

4

The Middle of the Lesson

After reading this chapter, you should be able to

- Distinguish new information as either declarative or procedural knowledge in order to support teachers' instructional decision making.
- Advise teachers on ways students might use thinking skills to apply declarative knowledge.
- Advise teachers on ways students might practice and strategically apply procedural knowledge.
- Explain the wisdom behind teaching self-regulating skills and character traits.

TWO 13-YEAR-OLD BOYS, ANDREW AND ZACH, CHATTED IN THE BACK SEAT DURING carpool. They had some good things to say about school. For example, they complimented the new principal for having extended the lunch period and assigning top-shelf lockers to the 8th graders, making it easier to maneuver through the crowds that formed between class periods. They also liked the mobile classrooms away from the main building, because this gave them a chance to go outside.

But when the discussion turned to their actual classes, the tone changed to disenchantment. "Why do all of my classes have to be the same and so boring?" Andrew complained. "The teachers present their notes about what we're studying on the board or the overhead projector, or they sometimes give us a worksheet about the notes while they talk about them. That always takes half the class, and then the teachers make us sit there for discussion, or tell us to start our homework. . . ."

"Maybe high school will be different," Zach offered.

Certainly not all of the boys' classes are monotonous, but their perceptions should not be dismissed. The deficiency that the boys perceive is that their lessons are dull and don't stimulate thinking and learning. Why should this be, when teachers work so hard to plan good lectures with accompanying notes, activities for hands-on learning, and projects that involve student interaction?

Our subject in this chapter is the critical, content-focused "middle of the lesson." Using the Schema as a filter is a way for a principal to focus the discussion about the middle of the lesson on two essential operations: acquiring new information (N) and applying knowledge and skills (A). Of course, in an actual lesson, these operations often overlap, but for the purposes of lesson analysis and improvement, it can be very helpful to examine each separately. Do students understand how to gather and organize the content of the lesson well enough to retain it and apply it independently in new situations? Does the lesson incorporate enough practice time for students to learn procedures to automaticity so they can use them "without thinking"? A supervisor can recommend strategies to improve the middle of the lesson so that students like Andrew and Zach will find their classes both interesting and meaningful—and acquire the skills and deep understanding their teachers and principal intend.

Clarification of Some Technical Terminology

Let's begin by clarifying some terminology. Although this may seem pedantic, when the principal and teacher set out to improve student learning, it is helpful for them to use the same terms to distinguish nuances in the lessons.

First, *new information* learned in a class is defined as "what students will know" or "what students will know how to do"—in other words, the content of grade-level curriculum standards (benchmarks). We mentioned in Chapter 3 that when the principal and teacher discuss lessons or units of study, it is useful to identify whether the goal is to *know about* something such as the poems or legends of a group of people in a humanities class (declarative knowledge), or *know how to do* something such as use a barometer to measure rising or falling air pressure in a science class (procedural knowledge). Neurologists have found that the brain processes declarative and procedural knowledge differently. Educators who consider the distinction between the two types of knowledge have an advantage when it comes to lesson planning, because they can incorporate information-processing strategies appropriate to each type.

Figure 4.1 shows the distinction between declarative and procedural knowledge embedded in the Schema. At the beginning of the lesson, the observing principal should see that the teacher identifies the lesson goals (G) as *declarative and/or procedural curriculum* benchmarks. After a couple of minutes of cueing prior knowledge (A), the teacher presents the new declarative or procedural information (N) for the students to acquire.

Since students acquire declarative and procedural knowledge differently, we will refer to acquisition of declarative knowledge as *gathering facts and organizing* and acquisition of procedural knowledge as *following instructions and practicing*. We refer to gathering and organizing new declarative knowledge as *lower-level processing* because it refers loosely to important activities that actively help students acquire knowledge (such as using an organizer) as opposed to *higher-order processing*, which generally refers to applying a robust *thinking skill*. For procedural knowledge, *lower-level processing* involves the learner following steps or instructions and practicing them until the procedure can be executed automatically. *Higher-order processing* refers to knowing how and when to strategically employ a learned procedure in new situations.

During the middle of a lesson, an observing principal should see that the teacher planned for students to acquire new knowledge by choosing specific instructional methods that involve gathering, organizing, and shaping knowledge. Feedback strategies should definitely be evident as students are directed to partner, stop to check understandings, or pause to generate questions about the new facts or the steps in the procedures. When the lesson transitions from new information (N) to applying (A), the principal may see the activity change from just organizing facts to using a thinking skill, or from following steps to using the skill in a new situation. The transition may be abrupt but more likely will be a subtle change.

	FIGURE 4.1 **Acquisition and Application of Knowledge**	
G	☐ Identify grade-level curriculum standards (declarative or procedural) ☐ Identify skills, such as gathering and organizing (process) ☐ Identify self-regulating skills ☐ Identify character traits	
A	☐ Cue/prompt (prior knowledge)	
N	**Acquire and Process New Information**	
	Declarative	**Procedural**

	☐ Gather
	   ↓ e.g., read, listen, view, experience,
	     touch, taste, smell
	☐ Organize
	   ↓ e.g., take notes, use a graphic
	     organizer
		☐ Gather
		   ↓ e.g., read steps, listen to steps,
		     view a demonstration, experience
		☐ Practice
		     e.g., shape and modify to
		     automaticity

A	**Use Higher-Order Processing Skills**	

	☐ Apply a thinking skill
	     e.g., solve a problem, make a
	     decision, compare, analyze
		☐ Apply a procedure strategically, in a new
		     situation

G	☐ Review or score grade-level curriculum standards (declarative or procedural) ☐ Review or score self-regulating skills ☐ Review or score character traits	

In the next section, we define the declarative-procedural terminology in more detail because we believe that it really is a way to help a principal or coach recommend ways to plan and deliver instruction in a manner that will help students perform better.

Types of Knowledge: Declarative and Procedural

In a famous surgery in the late 1950s, patient "H. M." submitted to having his hippocampi extricated, resulting in the inhibition of his ability to process new declarative knowledge (factual information). Upon recovery, however, he could still perform procedural or habitual skills, such as playing the piano. What was learned from the surgery on H. M. may have contributed to other case studies that spawned nearly five decades of research on memory and led to insight on how humans make memories. This information applies directly to educators today.

Realizing that declarative knowledge could be lost while procedural knowledge remained intact (and vice versa) led specialists to distinguish between types of memory when considering patient performance. As educators we can extend our knowledge of behaviorist psychology and neuroscientific research to schools; it is useful to distinguish between the two types of knowledge in the curriculum. This means supervisors can assist teachers in planning or modifying instruction to accommodate the targeted type of learning.

Think about a bicycle. If you can name the parts of a bicycle (e.g., spokes, seat, brakes, gears), you have declarative knowledge, or knowledge that you can declare. If you can ride the bicycle, you have procedural knowledge, also known as habitual knowledge.

Now, let's complicate the situation. When you took the Bikes 101 course, you read a lot about bicycles, watched videos about biking, and practiced thinking about and answering questions about what you would do if you found yourself stranded with a busted bike. Later, when you experienced a problem while riding your new bike, you had an idea about how to fix it by making connections in your brain to the information you had learned. What you knew about bikes helped you solve the problem. In other words, you learned about bikes in two steps: (1) given facts about bikes, you processed these by gathering and organizing the information; and (2) you went on to apply this information using a cognitive strategy: problem solving. Declarative knowledge is "easy to learn and easy to forget," so we use two levels of processing skills—first, gathering and organizing information (lower-level) and second, applying or using thinking skills to help us make necessary connections and, in turn, remember the information better (higher-level). In Bikes 101, you processed as much information as possible and applied thinking skills in each situation so that you would be prepared to apply the knowledge when you needed to construct a new idea or solution.

Procedural knowledge is the "learning to ride the bike" part of our bike analogy. The way to learn to ride well is to practice riding (lower-level processing); the more you practice, the better you ride. Once you have decent riding skills, you use these skills in new situations (higher-level processing). For example, you may ride off-road, take a ride down a mountain, or even ride on ice. To fix the bike also requires procedural knowledge: the more often you replace a flat tire, the more proficient you become at switching it out quickly and efficiently. Procedural knowledge takes a bit of time to acquire (hard to learn, but hard to forget), but you can make progress by applying what you've mastered in new situations.

The reality is that we use both types of knowledge. When you needed to fix your bike, you used what you knew about bikes and the situation (declarative), but you had to have the skill set (procedural) to fix it. When we learn or wish to improve, we can deconstruct tasks to specify the type of knowledge, so as to identify a strategy that works best.

Declarative and Procedural Curriculum

Supervisors can help teachers determine where and how to improve learning by clarifying declarative and procedural knowledge within the curriculum and then coaching teachers to use strategies appropriate to each kind of learning.

In all subjects, teachers teach both kinds of knowledge; however, depending on the grade level, the course, and the requirements at a given point in a unit of study, teachers do emphasize declarative or procedural knowledge so that they can accurately assess student performance and give feedback for improvement. For efficiency reasons, we suggest a simple code to indicate the intended emphasis (declarative or procedural knowledge) on curriculum documents. A declarative benchmark for high school civics class might read, "*Understands* the effectiveness of limited and unlimited governments on personal freedom and collective decision making." An elementary language arts procedural benchmark might read, "*Decodes* unknown words using context clues."

Coding curriculum benchmarks as declarative or procedural gives both supervisors and teachers guidance that does not exist in most curriculum documents. Note the practicality of using the terms *understands* or *knows* to preface a declarative statement and the specific verb *decodes* to preface the procedural statement. When *understands* or *knows* prefaces a benchmark for a lesson, that benchmark is immediately recognizable as declarative knowledge; hence, the principal should observe the teacher teaching students to gather or organize facts and then apply a thinking skill. The terms *understands* and *knows* should trigger a mental model of a drop-down menu listing verbs ranging from low-level thinking (e.g., *identifies, recognizes, describes, explains*) to higher-order thinking (e.g., *analyzes, solves*). A declarative benchmark allows the teacher to make instructional decisions based on a broad variety of activities, as indicated by the thinking skills.

A benchmark that begins with verbs other than *understands* or *knows* is immediately recognizable as procedural knowledge that is contextual to that subject area. Examples would be *estimates* and *graphs* in math and *sings* in music. The principal should observe a teacher leading lessons that allow distributed practice sessions, which are best conducted periodically after the original single block of time in which students learn the procedure.

Supervisor Summary

Identifying the type of knowledge, declarative or procedural, that will be taught in a particular lesson will help determine the best strategies for helping students learn.

○ Assist teachers in coding curriculum benchmarks as either declarative (those that require students to gather and organize information in order to understand or know) or procedural (those that require students to follow steps and practice skills).

Acquiring Declarative Knowledge

An analysis of school curriculum gives evidence that students spend at least half of their academic time learning declarative knowledge, but as they progress from primary to secondary school, the balance leans heavily toward declarative knowledge, or factual information. Teachers should vary the ways they present information to be stored as declarative knowledge, such as show-ing movies, giving lectures, reading aloud, providing time for independent reading, and including appropriate experiential learning activities. Histori-cally, the approach for students to learn vast amounts of declarative knowledge included memorization. While extremely effective for short-term use, memo-rizing facts does not necessarily equip learners to use factual knowledge for long-term use efficiently. So students should learn to use strategies to gather and organize the information before they use it in a new situation to make it more meaningful.

We stated earlier that acquiring new information, the *N* step of GANAG, results in better learning when the teacher employs instructional methods to teach students how to process, or act upon, the new information in the cur-riculum benchmark. Because we all know how easy it is to forget details when listening to a lecture, reading, or watching a documentary, we *gather and orga-nize* information. In practice, a principal may see the *teacher actually doing the gathering and organizing* for the students while the students follow along. The principal should see the teacher model a strategy to teach students how to gather or organize independently. For example, when a teacher makes a graphic organizer and asks students to fill it in, it may take away from the opportunity that a student has to learn which type of organizer (e.g., a web or a cause-effect organizer) works best to display a certain set of facts. When watching students gather information, the principal should see the teacher give instructions to learners about how to evaluate sources for relevance, accuracy, or purpose, so the students can check themselves.

If a principal notes during a pre-observation conference that the students will acquire factual information by watching a video, then the principal should also observe the students engage in a process skill. If the teacher expects stu-dents to take notes during the film and then organize their notes in order to collaborate with other students to create a report or project, then the process skills of note taking and organizing information will need to be taught or reinforced.

Many resources about standards include skills such as these separately from the content standards and may refer to them as "process skills," as in the

New York State documents (www.nysed.gov). Process skills may seem to be a mix of skills, but they are teachable, assessable, and do help students learn the content more effectively than memorizing or taking verbatim notes. Some examples might include the following:

- Using active reading strategies across all subjects
- Gathering information from print and digital media
- Collecting and interpreting data
- Evaluating sources for relevance, accuracy, or purpose
- Taking notes and organizing information in a graphic organizer
- Communicating clearly for different audiences and purposes
- Working with others to achieve goals
- Performing various roles in a group to ensure better outcomes

A school can generate a list of process skills set up in a format similar to other curriculum documents: cantilevered by grade or cluster level, or even specified by subject area. In Syracuse City School District, Francine Grannell coaches teachers to adopt process skills across the content areas to support "rigor and relevance." Using strategies compiled by the International Center for Leadership in Education (www.leadered.com), she coaches teachers to teach students strategies such as *note taking, role-playing, using instructional technology*, and *questioning*.

Principals are likely to see that teachers do not necessarily plan to teach students to gather and organize declarative knowledge as separate tasks, so often the teachers are unable to provide corrective feedback for improvement. Also, principals may see teachers "taking shortcuts" in the interest of time to cover material. Strategies like these (distributing prepared notes or not allotting time for students to share or generate their own questions) cost learners in terms of knowledge retention. Depending on the age or grade level of the students, a principal may observe a teacher introducing, modeling, or prompting use of a process skill for students to implement when organizing declarative facts and concepts. This requires that the principal observe or discuss with the teacher the declarative content of the benchmarks and what strategy the students will use to gather and organize the information.

Supervisor Summary

When factual information is being taught, principals should also observe process skills being taught or reviewed. These skills equip students to gather facts and organize information.

- ○ Remind teachers that process skills include note taking, gathering information from media, evaluating sources for relevance and accuracy, and collecting and interpreting data.
- ○ Emphasize that when students effectively use process skills to learn new information, retention of learned knowledge is greatly increased.

The higher-order level of processing declarative information is using thinking skills. Because this part of processing is so critical to remembering and using information, we place it in the Schema under the step *apply*, the second *A* in GANAG.

Applying Declarative Knowledge: Thinking Skills

Sharon's husband, Gary, owns a business. When hiring employees, he has the same requirement for those with a high school diploma as he does for those with more schooling: they must be able to think and use situational cognition. Although the entry-level jobs may not imply independent thinking, advancement is granted to workers who demonstrate problem-solving solutions for everyday routines. When a cashier reorganizes consumer traffic to allow for less wait time, for example, or when the stock personnel change the schedules for receiving to accommodate perishable versus nonperishable goods, Gary provides recognition for this thinking and these accomplishments.

National calls for schools to teach and test thinking persist. Consider that the International Society for Technology in Education (ISTE) recommends teaching reasoning skills to all students in the updated National Educational Technology Standards (ISTE, 2008) as a requirement in the increasingly digital world. David Conley, director of the Center for Educational Policy Research at the University of Oregon, writes in *College Knowledge: What It Really Takes for Students to Succeed and What We Can Do to Get Them Ready* that "students who are confident critical thinkers can more easily formulate and express original ideas" (Conley,

2005, p. 81). These voices echo in the 21st century what Benjamin Bloom (1956) called for in *Taxonomy of Educational Objectives* some 50 years ago: Students must learn to think in order to apply learned information in new ways.

The ubiquitous calls for higher-order thinking skills and demands for more reasoning questions over recall ones in common assessments should lead a supervisor to observe how the teacher plans for students literally to learn to think and show their thinking on an assessment. Thinking skills are applied in order to know a topic more deeply and be able to generate original thought. Jane and her coauthors in *Classroom Instruction That Works* (Marzano et al., 2001) provided research showing that students who use the thinking skills of identifying similarities and differences, generating and testing hypotheses, and asking thoughtful questions improve retention and use of knowledge. When learners use thinking skills, they apply effort to reorganize facts and concepts to make personal sense of the information and generate new ideas. In doing so, they strengthen neural connections, and the effect is longer retention of the information.

In *Improving Student Learning One Teacher at a Time* (Pollock, 2007), thinking skills are organized around Bloom's taxonomy (see Figure 4.2). The thinking skills on the right side of the figure are the skills that should be explicitly stated in the GANAG lesson plan as the application (A) in the lesson.

The well-respected Primary Years Programme (PYP), designed by the International Baccalaureate Organization, explicitly embeds thinking skills (inquiry) as part of the unit planning framework. PYP Associate Regional Manager Corine Van den Wildenberg describes planning with teachers as "frontloading thinking for the learner." Every lesson deliberately prompts the teacher to address specific thinking skills during planning, delivery, and assessment.

In Jen Au Claire's secondary lesson about river valleys, she guides students to reorganize notes into a comparison matrix in order to compare three civilizations on the basis of different geopolitical characteristics. Because students may gather different sets of facts, they may reach varied conclusions as they make their comparisons. By separating the process of gathering new knowledge from the actual application of knowledge, Jen can give feedback to learners about the relationship between the amount and quality of facts they collected and the accuracy or creativity of their conclusions.

FIGURE 4.2
A Hierarchy of Thinking Skills

Taxonomy Level	Specific Thinking Skills
Knowledge	Recall (facts or method)
	Classify
Comprehension	Conceptualize
	Predict (if, then)
Application	Compare
	Make an analogy
Analysis	Express a point of view
	Identify a system or structure
Synthesis	Form and test a hypothesis
	Solve a problem
Evaluation	Make a decision
	Argue or persuade
	Make a judgment or critique

Terry Osman, an Advanced Placement teacher, created a standard in his school's social studies curriculum that included explicit thinking skills, including *questioning to find clarity* and *structuring arguments*. The students learn the skills and are expected to use them throughout the year; Terry consistently gives the students feedback on the use of the skills themselves and on whether or not the application of the skills is helping students learn the content of the units of study more efficiently.

Type "thinking or reasoning skills" into an Internet search engine, and you will find numerous compilations that are well supported by research. The lists include skills such as predicting, inferring, problem solving, and investigating. Each of these skills can be further defined by the steps that one follows in order to complete the thinking process. An elementary principal might encourage teachers in the building to collaborate to generate a set of skills for use in the school since the thinking skills require practice over many years.

It is critical to see that students learn how to use these skills to generate new ideas or draw conclusions in order to have a better understanding of the information. Principals collaborating with teachers or observing classrooms should be able to see students talking about the thinking skills that they are using in the class.

Supervisor Summary

Supervisors need to distinguish the separate processes of gathering facts and applying knowledge, and ensure that teachers empower students to use higher-level thinking skills in declarative knowledge application.

- Look for students to demonstrate thinking skills—such as predicting, problem solving, analyzing, and inferring—as indications that they are applying higher-level reasoning to generate new ideas that expand upon factual information covered in class.
- Assist teachers in your school to generate process skills and thinking skills documents similar to subject area documents.

Acquiring and Applying Procedural Knowledge

Unlike processing declarative knowledge, when the benchmark for a lesson is procedural knowledge, the principal should see students "practicing." The introduction of procedural knowledge requires presentation of a skill; the equivalent process skill is to practice between learning each new step with corrective feedback to make improvements. Once students achieve a level of proficiency, they can shape skills to make them their own and apply the procedures in new situations. Referring back to Figure 4.1 (see page 82), one can see that to process procedural knowledge at a lower level, the learner *follows and practices steps to gain automaticity*; to process procedural knowledge at a higher level, the learner *applies these steps strategically in new situations*.

Principal Tony Cardamone observes that teaching procedural knowledge constitutes a change in the Schema framework, and we agree. He states that when teachers identify procedural benchmarks in a lesson, the Schema really appears as "GANananAG"—set the curriculum goal, access prior knowledge, teach a few steps, apply or practice briefly, add more steps or some declarative knowledge, practice, and repeat, until the lesson is concluded.

Tony also notes that when the students are practicing procedural benchmarks over a period of a few days, they are not engaged in acquiring new information. Therefore, for the 5- or 10-minute practice sessions that may occur daily, it is not necessary to adhere religiously to the Teaching Schema for Master Learners to generate good lessons for teaching procedural knowledge. Again, we concur.

When the principal and teacher together determine that the objectives of a lesson are procedural, then the activities for the lesson should include both massed and distributed practices. The teacher should guide these practice sessions by modeling and demonstrating each part of the procedure and systematically increasing intensity and complexity. A principal may ask the teacher to identify when procedural strategies will be taught over a series of lessons or units and how students will receive formative feedback to learn procedures to the point of automaticity. Then, during observations, the principal should see evidence of students tracking their own performances, effectively obtaining and using formative feedback from the teacher, and trying new steps or strategies through opportunities provided by the teacher.

The litmus test for procedural knowledge is whether the learner can use the procedure "without thinking." It seems ironic that we teach students not to think about procedural knowledge, but that is the nature of learning useful habitual behaviors.

Supervisor Summary

When the supervisor and teacher determine that benchmarks represent procedural knowledge, the supervisor should observe students practicing the newly learned skills.

- Ensure practice sessions for students begin with and are intermittently guided by teacher demonstration.
- Look for evidence that students are obtaining and using feedback to adjust their steps or strategies of practice and tracking their own performance.

Self-Regulating Skills

We have discussed declarative and procedural knowledge and how to process or practice the information to make it more memorable. A powerful set of skills, the self-regulating strategies help us to gain intelligence, achieve academically, and succeed in school and in life. In addition to making decisions and solving problems, students who perform well at self-regulating skills are often described by an ambiguous set of characteristics that address *how* a student responds to learning and applying knowledge, articulated using terms such as *responsible, determined,* or *reflective.* Some will argue that these characteristics can be taught through modeling and reinforcement; others disagree. But most agree that employers and colleges expect to find these traits in graduates with 12 or more years of schooling.

We decided to address these skills in this section for two reasons. As students learn new information, their effort can significantly improve their chances of accomplishment. In *Classroom Instruction That Works* (Marzano et al., 2001), Jane and her coauthors point out that most students are not aware of the impact of effort on achievement and that students can learn to change their beliefs and, therefore, their performances. Because these skills are assessed by teachers under the heading of effort or work habits on report cards, we suggest that students can be taught to do them better and, in the long run, improve performance across all subjects. For an excellent source on skills such as these, read the *Habits of Mind* book series by Arthur L. Costa and Bena Kallick (2000).

Some other authors distinguish between self-regulating skills and character traits. Self-regulating skills may include *showing respect, punctuality, responsibility, resilience,* and *perseverance.* Character traits may include *compassion, tolerance, citizenship, integrity,* and *positive attitude.* A useful distinction between the groups is that self-regulating skills can generally be taught through a set of steps with corrective feedback, whereas character traits are difficult to prescribe as steps but can be learned through modeling or viewed in exemplary behaviors. In either case, learners can improve both self-regulating performances and demonstrate strong character, and both can affect overall learning and performance.

One extremely important issue related to feedback and improvement also involves a self-regulating skill. Research in *Classroom Instruction That Works* (Marzano et al., 2001) suggests that students should learn to track themselves on applying self-regulating skills by using rubrics to describe their levels of performance. When students perform content-based tasks, they can self-assess how well they perform the self-regulating skills and how that impacts their overall performance. The data give them an idea whether they need to improve their effort or knowledge, or both.

Because these skills strongly affect how well students will cognitively respond to the middle of a lesson, a principal can guide a teacher to include role modeling and performance tracking of skills such as these in order to ensure that acquiring and applying new information is a robust and meaningful task for all learners. The principal may even decide to lead the school or a curriculum team in identifying these self-regulating skills and character traits.

As Sharon and her colleagues note, "Learning is the improvement of student knowledge, skill, and disposition" (Martin et al., 1997, p. 389). It is the responsibility of the school to find ways to improve all three of these factors. In this chapter, we have discussed the components separately but stress that the relationship among them is essential for making long-term memories and generating good work.

Supervisor Summary

Self-regulating skills and character traits permeate all learning and expression of both declarative and procedural knowledge. These nonacademic skills are expected by employers and colleges and contribute to success in life.

○ Collaborate with teachers to create strategies for helping students develop these self-regulating skills and character traits.

○ Look for evidence of student attitudes, effort, responsibility, and respectfulness learned through modeling or steps taught by the teacher.

To summarize, principals can affect students' learning by working with teachers to clarify the type of knowledge being conveyed in a lesson, either declarative or procedural, and the strategy that works best for learning it. If the curricular objectives are declarative, then planning for and delivering information should include blocks of time for students to acquire and apply knowledge. If the curricular objectives are procedural, the lessons may be planned more like "chunked" learning, in which the learner gains the knowledge of steps, practices, and repeats the process. In either case, the principal can recommend that teachers teach process and self-regulating skills to learners to help them learn better.

Supervisor Voice

Monique Conway, Middle School Principal

During the first phone call from Monique, we recognized that the addition of the Teaching Schema for Master Learners to the combination of leadership and dedicated staff at her Los Angeles-area middle school would change business as usual with regard to student performance.

An Exciting Challenge

In July 2005, when I began my assignment as a new principal with the Rialto Unified School District in California, I found myself rejoicing in my heart and soul . . . but also shaking in my boots. My charge was to lead a school of 1,400 students out of Program Improvement Status. The climate and staff morale were about what you would expect in an underperforming school anticipating budgets cuts that would ultimately result in the layoff of 10 staff members. The comportment and attitude of our diverse group of 6th though 8th graders—culled from different neighborhoods and brought together through busing—left much to be desired, and struggles to manage student behavior added to staff frustration. Some teachers found themselves focusing more on student behavior than on student learning. Others, veterans of a series of improvement initiatives enacted over the years, had lost hope that it was possible to realize real gains in student achievement.

It soon became obvious to me that changing schedules and amassing more learning materials was not going to help improve student learning. As the principal, it was critical that I focus my efforts on improving teachers' instructional practices. To be more specific, I needed to focus my time and support on improving the quality of *each* teacher's instructional practice.

My classroom observations had shown me that direct instruction was the predominant instructional method being used and that there was little active student participation in learning activities. My administrative team and I considered the needs of our staff in order to change instructional approaches and the needs of students to show gains in academic achievement. We decided to invite Jane Pollock to meet with our teachers, and the assistance she provided them in learning about implementing the Big Four and the Teaching Schema for Master Learners helped us to see positive changes.

From Skepticism to Enthusiasm

When Jane began meeting with our staff, many teachers attended the meetings reluctantly and were skeptical about implementing new strategies. Jane emphasized the importance of focusing feedback to curriculum targets and structuring lessons around the Schema steps referred to as GANAG. She discussed with us the positive differences that occur when students receive ongoing feedback and are active participants in the learning process.

Some teachers wanted to transition to this new approach gradually, and others wanted to begin immediately with major changes in their procedures. Our ELL coach was one of the "immediate changers." When he discussed the feedback technique that Jane had presented, he became excited about the results he was seeing with students and began working to help other teachers more fully utilize this practice. The interest began to spread among the staff, and soon, many teachers admitted that they were beginning to shift their instructional approach toward the Schema. After I began meeting with the language arts teachers and supporting the use of the Schema as a framework for their program, teachers from that department began to stop by my office to show me assessment results and to discuss decisions for their next instructional steps based on insight those results provided them. Now, during planning meetings, teachers are putting more effort into focusing on curriculum objectives and learning goals.

I find that, as a supervisor, the Schema provides me with tools for working more effectively and collegially with my teachers. As we plan and discuss lessons together, it is evident that teachers appreciate the support that I can offer through effective feedback that is focused clearly on practice. I am observing more passion for teaching and learning evolving or reinventing itself in each teacher.

Voices From Our Staff

Brent is a teacher on my staff who is among those who are excited about the new approach to teaching and learning that is quickly becoming a part of our school culture. When we first began to implement the Schema and GANAG, Brent found change to be difficult, and the positive feelings that he now has about the Schema and its use in planning and teaching emerged from initial frustration in trying something new. It was the improvement in student learning that the use of GANAG brought about that "clinched the deal" for Brent. As he states, "I feel that I have found a tool that will help my teaching truly focus on learning rather than behavior modification. Besides, I believe when students realize that they are learning, their behavior will no doubt improve."

Brent is sharing the student success he is observing with other teachers, and he is also encouraging students to share with each other what they are learning. This is a big step considering the passive nature of "learning" that was occurring in classrooms prior to our use of the Schema, and the previous heavy focus on improving student behavior in our school. In Brent's words, "A big change in my teaching this year has been the focus on student collaboration. My class now incorporates a great amount of academic discussion by using pair-shares, jigsaws, and groupings . . . students enjoy this environment more."

Ted was a teacher in our school before accepting an administrative position at another location. He found the strategies and conversations exchanged in our staff development meetings after adopting the Schema to be "truly life changing." For Ted, one of the most powerful components of the Schema-initiated change was the use of classroom technology like the electronic grade book, specifically, "upgrading the recordkeeping software to include standards monitoring for grading, which increases the efficacy of feedback for both teacher and students." Now in a new administrative position within our district, Ted has stated that he is anxious to share with his staff the research about teaching and learning that Jane shared with us.

A Satisfying Journey

We are now in the fourth year of my principalship in our "much-improved" middle school. We met our schoolwide academic performance index (API) target, and the students enrolled in our English language and resource specialist programs showed incremental growth. The progress we've made is the catalyst we need to continue our work to improve student learning.

Our improvement has come as a result of working together and focusing on research-based strategies that benefit teachers and students. We continue to face the litany of challenges that most schools face, but our teachers are focused and remain convinced that student learning is our primary goal and that the Schema is a wonderful tool that assists all of us in improving student learning. It has truly been a satisfying journey for this one principal working with one teacher at a time.

5

The End of the Lesson

After reading this chapter, you should be able to

• Explain why it is beneficial for students to review learning goals and judge their understanding or performance through peer, teacher, and self-evaluation.

• Reinforce with teachers the importance of providing students ongoing feedback about their progress toward curriculum benchmarks.

• Recommend strategies for prompting students to generalize or summarize learning concepts and procedures at the end of the lesson.

IF THERE ARE SOME CLASSES THAT BEGIN WITH "BOOM! WE'RE IN IT!" (TO QUOTE ANDY Jones, a principal in New London, Wisconsin), then there are also classes that end with equally inauspicious abruptness: "Oops! There's the bell!"

Neurologist and classroom teacher Judy Willis has noted that the summary at the end of a lesson is "dendrite food," because it strengthens connections and helps learners grow new dendrites (2006, p. 86). Other neurologists refer to neurons "stabilizing" after key learning connections are made (Doidge, 2007, p. 80). The end of the classroom lesson, according to the Teaching Schema for Master Learners, is *generalizing*, the final *G* in GANAG. In this chapter, we discuss how principals can suggest strategies to help teachers improve the ends of lessons.

Although all parts of the Schema allow and even encourage verbal or written feedback, the end of the lesson is one final time for students to check their understandings, performances, or perceptions related to the benchmarks articulated at the lesson's beginning. Similarly, all parts of a lesson planned with the Schema can include opportunities for teachers to check student understanding through activities such as "table talks" or "shows of hands," but the end of the lesson gives teachers one final chance to informally assess both individual improvement as well as group progress. The decision to record learning progress in the form of scores or grades at this time in a lesson is left to the teacher. It may be that scores are documented for some students and not for others.

To this point, we have focused on the instructional aspect of the Schema; now we begin to emphasize the original tenet that instruction and assessment complement one another in the classroom.

The Who and Why of Generalizing

Many teachers ask why the Schema calls for concluding a lesson with *generalizing* instead of using the more familiar term *closure*. The first reason is that most teachers who do conscientiously plan for closure at the end of lessons summarize the learning *for* their students, and we want to be sure that teachers recognize that we are suggesting that they do something different. Amanda Haynes, a 6th grade teacher, asked us, "But isn't that what we are supposed to do? I thought it was my job to summarize what we learned that day so that students would leave with that review of the goals for the lesson." Our answer was yes and no. Yes, it's important to have a review of the lesson's goals to support students' self-assessment of the progress they made during class, but it's the *students* who should do the summarizing or generalizing, not the teacher.

The second reason we focus on generalizing as opposed to "providing closure" is that we like to think of generalizing in a technical way. A learner who understands a generalization, as opposed to knowing a fact or set of organized facts, is equipped with a more efficient kind of cognitive currency. Educators tell us that when students are involved in the lesson summarization or generalization processes, they are much more likely to remember what they have learned and to practice or apply their knowledge independently. If lesson generalization is performed by the teacher, without student involvement, students have little cause to reflect on their progress and are not stimulated to question how they might meaningfully apply learned information.

When it comes to explaining the value of generalizing at the end of a lesson, the "putting the tab on the folder" metaphor resonates with Jami Kohl, principal at Franklin Elementary School. By directing students to score themselves to the benchmarks or summarize their understandings of the topics for the day, teachers' guidance allows the students to "close the lesson" rather than letting the class period dissolve into social activities. Jami notes that when she observes consecutive days of a class, if students have generalized or summarized the previous day, they seem to open mental folders using the tabs on the subsequent days of the unit.

Jami further describes the generalization at the end of a lesson as a way to discuss formative assessment with teachers when conferencing. "When we discuss formative assessment," she says, "most teachers imagine another test. But using the phrase *formative assessment* with the end-of-the-lesson generalization cues a different instructional behavior. It implies that a teacher needs to gather more information about student performances in order to make a meaningful judgment." In other words, the teacher may think, "I have more teaching to do, since not all of my students have hit the mark yet" or, "They have all hit the mark and are now ready to move on."

Supervisor Summary

Students, rather than the teacher, should summarize or generalize learned information.

○ Emphasize to teachers that summarizing and generalizing allows students to create "tabs" on their mental folders that they can open the next day to expand upon or practice what they have learned.

○ Champion student-led generalizing as a way for teachers to assess student progress and improve planning for the next lesson.

A Note About Formative and Summative Assessment

The term *formative assessment* must return to our discussions as we turn from the exclusive focus on summative measures called for by a national movement designed to organize statewide tests and move toward expanded efforts to "mind the gap"—that is, improve learning through daily classroom assessment. Historically, we have progressed from assessing individual intelligence for the purpose of improving education to realizing that improving instructional practices is the way to foster the highest potential of each student.

In his research on program evaluation, Michael Scriven made a distinction between formative assessment and summative assessment, indicating that the meanings of the terms differed by "form" and "sum" (Borg & Gall, 1983, p. 758). He stated that formative assessment is conducted for the purpose of "forming" while the program is still being developed; summative assessment functions to evaluate the program or product after it has been fully developed. Summative assessment is often used to compare competing programs or products. When transferred to students in classrooms, this differentiation supports formative assessment for the purpose of "forming" the learning through and during instruction, and summative assessment as the evaluation after learning that is often used for comparison purposes. Feedback targeted to curriculum benchmarks is the means by which we "form" the learning progression toward these developmentally appropriate aims.

Supervisor Summary

Formative assessment promotes learning when used to give feedback to students about progress toward curriculum targets.

○ Throughout and by the end of a lesson, look for evidence that the teacher gathers and shares information about student progress.

○ Suggest to teachers that summative assessment measures be used after a given block of learning is complete.

Strategies for Varying Lesson Endings

Varied instructional approaches stimulate greater learning (Ford, Muth, Martin, & Murphy, 1996). Many teachers admit to us that ending a lesson is not an instructional strength for them, but they state that they would be willing to change their lesson endings if they knew of more strategies to incorporate into the last three to five minutes of a class—strategies that will keep students motivated and energized and will incorporate generalization. Bonnie Van Benschoten, principal at Durgee Middle School, told us that one of her teachers pleaded with her: "Please help me end my class with any strategy but the exit ticket!" To this end, we brainstormed a list of strategies supervisors like Bonnie might recommend and categorized them to make them easier to use. The final group of anecdotal strategies, beginning at the bottom of page 106, was submitted to us by teachers and supervisors.

Paper-and-Pencil Strategies

Summarizing or drawing conclusions. Before putting away their interactive notebooks for the day, students can write a summary or draw a conclusion about the learning, specifically restating the objectives or benchmarks. This is an effective strategy to use when students have used a specific thinking skill during a lesson, because it allows them to record synopses or general findings as journal entries. Gary Nunnally, a high school social studies teacher, shows students how to organize the notebook so summaries for daily lessons can be combined later as key components for the summary of the unit.

Self-scoring. Using the list of benchmarks the teacher provides at the beginning of the lesson or unit, the students can self-assess or score themselves and keep track of the progress throughout the lesson and the unit, following a form like the one Gail Goff uses (see Figure 3.1, p. 64).

Index card progressions. Each student can write a summary for the day's lesson on a large index card. This is repeated on the same card each day for three or four days, as different objectives are addressed for that benchmark. Some teachers ask students to use the index card to start the summary and then pass it to partners or team members to add to the conclusion.

Questions. If the teacher started the lesson by providing cues or questions, then students are given the opportunity to generate written questions that they may still have about a topic. These questions may be used the next day to open the lesson.

Vocabulary tickets. The teacher in Bonnie Van Benschoten's school is right that the exit ticket shouldn't be any teacher's sole strategy, but as part of a collection of strategies, exit-ticket-style activities are definitely effective. In this one, students leave the classroom only after submitting a sticky note on which each has written a new academic vocabulary term (such as *perpendicular, simile, imperialism,* or *alto*) that he or she feels ready to use independently.

Computer-Assisted Strategies

Class comments. Students can access the class Web site to add comments in the section for the day. High school English teacher Jeff See uses this tactic to create a venue to provide feedback to learners and also benefit from immediate feedback from individual students, so he can adjust instruction accordingly.

E-mail wrap-ups. Students can send an e-mail to the teacher assessing their learning status or asking questions about the lesson. Instructional technology coordinator Melissa Julian encourages students to use a program on her district's Web site that allows students to communicate with teachers using various sources; e-mail gives teachers a way to organize the responses.

Blogging the lesson. Students can post an entry to a class blog. When students use a wiki or a blog, their classmates are privy to the summaries or questions as well, creating a conversation in which the entire class can participate.

Charting progress. With brief instruction on how to create an electronic spreadsheet with the benchmarks, students may use time at the end of the lesson to document and track their assignment scores and consider the trends.

Tech-assisted summarizing. Students can use software programs that take notes and summarize them (such as Inspiration), and then share the summaries with peers.

Partner Strategies

Pair-sharing. Students can team up with a classmate to restate the lesson's objectives or benchmarks in their own words and talk through their understanding of the content.

Summary exchange. Students can find another person in the room who agrees with their summary of the topic; if they write out the summaries, they can add details to each other's work.

Collective summarizing. Students, in groups, can write a summary of the major understandings and select one student to write the summary on the board for the class to discuss.

Walking summaries. Students line up by twos as they walk to specials, lunch, or recess and discuss the lesson just concluded. When Jon Langstaff employs this strategy with his 3rd graders, he walks alongside pairs of students and gives them feedback on the accuracy of their understandings.

"Two stars and a wish." Students share what they have learned in the lesson and then agree to "two stars and a wish": two important new facts, skills, or understandings acquired, and a statement or comment about something else they would like to learn. This strategy is a favorite of Daniel Todd, an assistant principal at the International School of Kampala, Uganda.

Physical Representation Strategies

Traffic light feedback. In this informal gauge of student understanding, the teacher posts a "traffic light" of three construction-paper circles, which students use to self-report on their level of understanding or mastery. Brian Holzman, a physical education teacher, tells us that he has a "traffic light" of three circles posted on the doorway, and as the students leave the room, they hit the green ("I got it!"), yellow ("Almost!"), or red ("Need more practice!") as he watches.

Hand signaling. In a similar technique, students use a hand signal such as "thumbs up," "thumbs to the side," or "thumbs down" to indicate their level of understanding of topics or procedures. Because this is nontextual, students in the primary grades or even prekindergarten can readily use this strategy.

Anecdotal Strategies

Homework review. Kristie Lyon, a high school math teacher, shares that one of her strategies is to occasionally use the previous night's homework review as the generalization step (rather than as a chapter-opening strategy to help students access prior knowledge). She finds it a good way to supplement the conceptual understandings of math practices; sometimes, the students just need practice before moving on to new steps.

Closure of choice. When elementary school teacher Camille Leisten asks her students to review their goals at the end of the lesson, she gives them choices to facilitate their engagement. Any of the strategies work, she says, so she may end a lesson by indicating to students that they can either write a summary in the learning log, make an exit card with a question on it, or use a scoring card to show their understandings.

"Click and save." George Santos, who teaches computer courses at Carol Morgan School in the Dominican Republic, asks students to metaphorically "click and save" the day's lesson. At the end of the lesson, he asks students to review the work they accomplished for the day and verbally "click and save" what they will need for the future.

"The Peabody Box of Operations." During the final minutes of class, secondary math teacher David Peabody has his students take out a large index card and mark the corners with the symbols for math operations: +, −, ×, and %. He asks students to write about the day's learning using one of the operations as a cue; for example, "The problems we did today really helped me *increase* (multiply) my ability to solve for an unknown" or "I'm still not understanding the *difference* (subtract) between associative and commutative." Students turn in their "Peabody boxes" to the teacher as they leave class. This strategy serves both student self-evaluation and teacher assessment of progress.

Sloganeering. Edwina Hay, an 8th grade English teacher, likes to have students summarize the basic concept of a lesson by writing a bumper sticker or a vanity plate for a car. For example, when they are studying editing, a student might write, "Thesaurus—to explain a 'dinosaurus,' use a thesaurus."

Kagan Cooperative Learning Structures. Dana Paykos, the supervisor of curriculum and instruction at Rancocas Valley Regional High School in New Jersey, noticed that the ends of lessons were areas where teachers appreciated hearing new suggestions. He trains teachers to utilize Kagan Cooperative Learning Structures (www.kaganonline.com) to help students process their content understandings and notes that many of these structures work well to improve the ends of lessons as well as other parts of GANAG. The structures have catchy titles (such as "RallyRobin" and "Kagan RoundTable") and very clear directions, so students learn to generalize quickly and efficiently.

Supervisor Summary

A supervisor with a large repertoire of lesson endings to share with teachers can greatly promote student learning.

○ Be familiar with the various lesson endings in the five categories identified. During pre-observation conferences, collaboratively plan with teachers which ending strategy to use for a given lesson.

○ In classroom observations, look for the teacher to gather information about student progress through the use of an appropriate lesson ending.

○ In the post-observation conference, discuss the information the teacher gathered from the ending activity and how the teacher can best use this for instructional planning.

A principal who encourages a teacher to provide the learning goal at the beginning of the lesson helps ensure that each subsequent activity in that lesson presents an opportunity for formative assessment or feedback. Giving students information about their progress while accessing prior knowledge, moving to new information, actively applying the knowledge, or generalizing at the end of a lesson is essential to achieving the curricular end results that both teachers and students desire. The supervisor who champions "forming" learning for all students can support teachers' efforts in this area by making sure that all teachers have viable curriculum targets, know how to employ a diverse array of feedback methods, and capitalize on the opportunity the end of the lesson provides to link feedback to those curriculum targets.

Supervisor Voice

Jeff Farrington, High School Principal

When Canadian teacher Jeff Farrington began teaching middle school science at the American School Foundation of Monterrey in Monterrey, Mexico, he marveled that "learning was learning," as he taught students from around the world. In a few years, when he became a secondary principal, he was able to share the techniques he had learned in the classroom with others.

What Is a Good Teacher?

I was fortunate to learn early in my administrative career that efforts to improve student learning are closely linked to teacher efficacy. However, in my first years as an administrator, it was much too easy to get bogged down with "administrivia," such as budgets, timetables, discipline issues, and the ever-increasing daily "to do" list that kept me in the office and away from the classrooms. Despite these distractions, I never lost sight of the fact that the teacher is the element of education with the most potential to make the greatest impact on learning. Because my new role had me in a position to "make change happen" through other people, my question became "What is a good teacher?"

The easy answer was the classic argument pitting the art of teaching against the science of teaching. Many great teachers receive accolades such as "He just has it," or "She was born with it." Many teachers excel at the craft, and some say "it" cannot be taught. To me, this argument seemed to be a cop-out, making teacher supervision a sorting process rather than a development process. Therefore, my journey began with learning the definition of "it" and how "it" could be developed and evaluated in teachers.

Seeking "It" and Finding the Schema

As the principal of an international school, I experience higher staff turnover than at a regular stateside school, so I was looking for a broad-based supervision model that would work with my teachers. I enrolled in a course called "Instructional Supervision" given by the Principals' Training Center for International Leadership. The course covered various supervision models outlining the criteria for effective teaching. Charlotte Danielson's *Enhancing Professional Practice: A Framework for Teaching* (2007) piqued my interest. Danielson's framework clearly outlined criteria regarding professional practice and recommendations for a tracked model. This suited our school because we wished to formally observe all new staff in the first year of their contracts.

I pored over examples from Danielson's framework, the five core propositions of the National Board for Professional Teaching Standards (http://nbpts. org), and the competency "look fors" recommended by the Ontario Ministry of Education supervision document (www.edu.gov.on.ca/eng/teacher/appraise. htm). Blending the sources, I began to delineate exactly what it was that we generally expected from teachers regarding effective teaching that would, in turn, lead to improved student learning.

Once the criteria for effective professional practice were in place, my energy was focused on the *science* of learning. What strategies proven to improve student learning could be taught and replicated in all teachers' classrooms? Our task turned to choosing instructional methodologies, providing staff development for implementation of these methodologies, and then monitoring their use in the classroom. That was when I read about the Teaching Schema for Master Learners.

As a teacher, I had never structured my lessons in this fashion. Each day, as students entered my classroom, I was greeted with a chorus of "What are we doing today, sir?" I knew where I was going (and often planned an entire quarter ahead), but I didn't make the learning targets overt to my students. Furthermore, the lesson-starter was a foreign concept to me, and lesson closure was impossible because students were not aware of the target. The Schema lesson design made sense to me as both a teacher and a supervisor, so I incorporated it into the instruction domain of our school's supervision document (see the figure on p. 112). With this new supervisory framework in hand, our administrative team set out to supervise instruction.

The Schema in our vision and goals. Our vision document included the goal of teaching "methodologies that promote higher-order thinking skills." To move from vision to action, the administrative team identified the following as one of our yearly goals: "Use the designated instructional Schema to ensure that we have consistency in our lesson planning and our teaching." As with any yearly goal, we then incorporated it into our staff development plan.

Training. The next step was not only to make staff aware of the goals for the year, but to provide in-service opportunities that would assist teachers in reaching the goal. At the beginning of each year, we outline the GANAG method for our new staff with the expectation that all teachers will use it. In addition, all of our internal in-service programs model the same format we expect teachers to use in their lessons with students.

The Schema's Role in Helping Teachers and Supervisors

In the early months of implementation, our staff focused solely on writing each day's lesson objectives targeted to curriculum standards on the board in their classrooms. Some teachers struggled with the difference between a concisely worded objective written from curricular targets (e.g., "understand metaphors as a literary device used by the author and provide examples") and a laundry list agenda (e.g., "hand in homework; hand back quiz; lab activity; homework questions"). By focusing on the steps of the Schema during planning and through administrator drop-in visits, we were able to track certain aspects of the Schema over time for each teacher. The key was to leave teachers with both positive feedback ("excellent closure activity") and constructive feedback ("missed your objective today" or "try to link the lesson objective with the curricular target, rather than putting up a to-do list"). We administrators wanted our observation feedback to translate to teachers' constructive feedback to learners. Furthermore, our observations provided a much more comprehensive approach with staff new to our school. By focusing on the steps of the Schema, we were able to participate with teachers in both lesson design and assessment.

At our school, we have experienced much success since the introduction of the Teaching Schema for Master Learners. We adapted our supervisory model

A Schema-Informed Supervision Framework

ELEMENT	Area of Concern	Approaches Standard	Meets Standard	Exceeds Standard
Setting the Learning Goal/ Objective	The lesson has no objective or the lesson activities do not demonstrate learning of the objective.	Teacher has a lesson objective, but it is not clear to students. The lesson activities match the objective.	Students are aware of the clearly defined objective around which the lesson activities are well organized.	Teacher has a clearly defined objective with explicitly linked lesson activities, allowing for reflection, assessment, and closure as appropriate.
Accessing Prior Knowledge	Teacher does not use students' past experience to lead directly into the lesson.	Teacher attempts to draw on past experience of students but is met with limited success.	Teacher links objective of the lesson well with students' past knowledge and experiences.	Each student is involved in using past experience (academic or real-life) to lead directly into the lesson. (Past experience matches the objective of the lesson.)
New Information Organized into Sub-objectives	Teacher does not break down or organize new information of lesson.	Lesson was divided into sub-objectives, but was not taught one sub-objective at a time, and new information was not organized.	Teacher presents new information one sub-objective at a time, which leads students toward achieving the objective of the lesson.	Teacher presents one sub-objective at a time, checking for understanding, and students process information using an advanced organizer.
Application of New Information	Teacher does not provide opportunities for students to apply new information.	Teacher's lessons are limited with respect to opportunities to apply information.	Teacher consistently makes attempts to have students use knowledge meaningfully with some sort of application skill.	Students use knowledge meaningfully by practicing skills in a new way or using complex reasoning to apply new information.
Active Engagement	Activities and assignments do not cognitively engage students. While students may be on task or active, they are not mentally engaged.	Some activities and assignments appropriately engage students mentally, but not all students are consistently (or simultaneously) involved.	Most activities and assignments actively engage students. Almost all students are simultaneously and consistently cognitively engaged in the lesson.	All students are cognitively engaged (simultaneously and consistently) in the activities of the lesson. Students initiate or adapt activities and projects to enhance understanding.
Closure/Summary	There is no summary of the lesson by the teacher or students.	Teacher summarizes lesson for the students.	Teacher involves each student in a summarizing activity regarding the content of the lesson.	Students overtly or covertly summarize the content of the lesson and match it to the main points of the lesson.

Source: Jeff Farrington, American School Foundation of Monterrey, Garza Garcia, Nuevo León, Mexico. Adapted from Danielson (2007) and Pollock (2007).

to incorporate the Schema, and teachers have become much more automatic about using it and making it part of our school's vernacular. For example, students now expect to see the lesson objective on the board; this practice has become standard operating procedure and part of our institutional memory. Some teachers list the objective as an essential question, so that closure of the lesson simply means having students answer the objective. Many of our teachers use a "primetime task" to access prior knowledge at the beginning of the lesson, instead of choosing a random attention-focusing activity.

One of the most remarkable changes we've observed is that more teachers actively plan for ways that students may apply their new information. This was our vision goal to increase. The application portion of the lesson provides students opportunities to do something with the information they have learned in order to understand it more profoundly and retain it longer.

Another significant change is that students now expect a closing at the end of every lesson—performed by them, not by the teacher. In feedback to a teacher, a 7th grade student wrote, "I like the end-of-lesson activity, as it allows me time to reflect on whether I got the objective or not." One teacher concludes each lesson with a generalization activity or an "at the very least I learned _____" cue tied to the objective. Other teachers use an exit ticket. Most important, teachers incorporate end-of-lesson activities as a holistic check for understanding and feedback for them to use in guiding future instruction.

I want to add, too, that all of our professional development sessions for teachers are now planned in the Schema's GANAG format. Not only do we on the administrative team benefit from using a very ordered lesson Schema as we plan, but the staff experience for themselves the effect these techniques have on learners. Finally, we have hired an instructional coach for the upcoming school year to assist in further implementation of the GANAG method. The method has become a very important part of our criteria for effective teaching and replication of best practices. Even though we believe we hire the best teachers, we know that our vision, our staff development, and our supervisory practices have an effect on helping teachers acquire the "it" that will improve student learning.

6

Improving the Plan Book and the Grade Book

After reading this chapter, you should be able to

• Explain the importance of using grade-level standards (benchmarks) as criteria for evaluating student performance and tracking progress.
• Help teachers align their grade book and plan book to improve communication and learning.
• Assist teachers in learning and implementing electronic record keeping in order to enhance communication with students, staff, and parents.

JENNIFER WEBER, AN ELEMENTARY TEACHER, CLUTCHED HER GREEN-PAPER GRADE BOOK. She peered at Jane suspiciously for a few moments and then admitted, "I can't show it to you; it would be showing you something really personal."

Although Jennifer had been observed at various times during her six years of teaching, no one had ever examined her grade book or asked her to bring it to a meeting with a supervisor. Jane went on to explain that a grade book can be a valuable means of supervisor–teacher communication and collaboration to improve learning. She wanted to model for Jennifer's principal how to give feedback to a teacher based on examining that teacher's grade book and plan book in tandem. If, for example, Jennifer's instructional plans included assessing two math benchmarks over three or four days, her principal might suggest she set up her grade book to track a few, benchmark-specific scores per student—possibly related to class work or quizzes. This kind of grading is called *criterion-based scoring* (Pollock, 2007).

In an e-mail reproduced in the Introduction to this book, Mike wrote that he appreciated the collaboration with his supervisor regarding instruction but believed that assessment had been overlooked in the observation and evaluation of his teaching. Mike wanted his principal to ask to see how well the students were performing (as documented in his grade book) and wished to discuss strategies to help students improve in specific areas (using his plan book). Principals who comfortably seek information about classroom data demonstrate to teachers the understanding that the classroom data are as critical as external data, perhaps because the classroom is where you affect learning. Collecting individual and whole-class data about learning progress, reorganizing the data relative to the curriculum criteria we refer to as benchmarks and objectives, and analyzing classroom data with a corroborating set of external data (such as state test scores) are critical to including assessment as an integral part of supervisory discussions.

Traditional Grading Practices

When we ask teachers and principals how many courses in their certification programs are focused on procedures and reasons for grading, their responses are revealing. They often mention a course or two on testing and evaluation but add that they learned next to nothing about tracking performance for the purpose of ensuring progress. Most learned what they know about grading and setting up grade books on the job—and without even the benefit of another teacher's mentorship. And almost all say that nowhere in their training did they explore research findings that daily and weekly scoring to benchmarks can be a powerful communication tool in support of improving student learning.

In general, grade book practices created or adapted by teachers often involve recording student performances using a scale or grade. Some of the patterns that we have recognized include the following:

• Many elementary teachers do not keep a traditional grade book; instead, they keep separate records or samples of student work in folders. They chart student progress only in specific content areas, such as reading.

• Many elementary teachers describe the weekend before report cards are due as laborious, because they generate "grades" or narratives based on weeks of performances that are organized by the chronology of activities.

• Most teachers score students on activities. A typical grade book (electronic or paper) displays a matrix in which the student name and scores are connected by dated activities. It is not unusual for a secondary teacher to document one score or grade per day for each student. Teachers categorize the scores as homework, quizzes, tests, projects, or participation.

• Many secondary teachers describe their grading process as "points based" and justify reporting summative grades as the number of points accrued. Sometimes the teachers adjust the grades based on behaviors, such as turning in work late or completing extra tasks for points. These teachers consider their grading methods to be efficient because a final grade is a precise calculation of an average of scores.

All of these practices are fairly effective at communicating a judgment to parents or guardians about how well a student is performing in school. However, because the traditional method for reporting student progress does not explicitly align with curriculum benchmarks, students tend to receive feedback that tells them "where they are" but not how to improve. It should be no surprise, then, that traditional grading and reporting practices do little to support student learning. Extensive examples of how these practices fall short can be found in publications by O'Connor (2002), Guskey and Bailey (2001), and Marzano (2000).

Benchmark-Based Grade Books

Rather than organizing scores in a grade book around the classic criteria like homework, participation, projects, tests, and quizzes, we recommend using benchmarks as categories in which to record data. In this way, the grade book maintains all of the scored observations or tasks but also tracks student progress over time to show trends in performance and *still* provides necessary data to consolidate into a single grade on a report card. A teacher whose grade book is organized by benchmarks is in a better position to match classroom performance data to the data collected by external measures, such as common assessments or state tests. In all of these cases, the principal and teachers can also use the data to drive decisions for differentiation and program modification.

In short, a grade book can and should be more than just a place to record data about student performance on sequenced projects and activities. If it is organized around curriculum benchmarks and aligned with the plan book, it can support student success by facilitating communication about student progress, allowing for achievement in benchmark areas to be corroborated with state test scores, and supporting more meaningful discussions between teacher and supervisor about assessment and instructional improvement.

To visualize how to set up a grade book to score to benchmarks instead of activities, imagine the standard, green-paper grade book with the student names down the left side and the little boxes across the top organized by weeks. Keep the student names where they are, but now imagine that instead of being labeled by weeks, each set of "weeks" is labeled as a benchmark. This leaves several boxes per benchmark in which to record scores (see Figure 6.1).

It is true that when teachers score by benchmarks, it's likely that there will be multiple scores per assignment. On the front end, this *is* more work, but when scores need to be calculated and reported, the teacher makes up the time. In addition, students perform better as a result of better feedback and the opportunity to analyze their scores for trends, not just missed assignments.

In *Improving Student Learning One Teacher at a Time* (Pollock, 2007), Chapter 5 is dedicated to the issues that teachers need to resolve once they decide to revise their grade books, including what to do about homework, how to grade effort, and how to determine which grading scale to use. As teachers begin to record these scores, they find themselves more aware of student strengths as well as areas where they can make changes to the lessons to help more students improve. Principals can work with teachers in these areas to improve opportunities schoolwide.

Teachers garner multiple benefits from setting up their grade books in this way, and many have transferred this practice to an electronic mode that offers more and different ways to analyze data and examine learning trends.

FIGURE 6.1

A Grade Book for Benchmark Scoring—Model 1

Student Names	Type the Benchmark Here						Type the Benchmark Here						Type the Benchmark Here						Type the Benchmark Here					
	Activity	Activity	Activity	Activity	Activity	Activity	Activity	Activity	Activity	Activity	Activity	Activity	Activity	Activity	Activity	Activity	Activity	Activity	Activity	Activity	Activity	Activity	Activity	Activity
Student 1																								
Student 2																								
Student 3																								
Student 4																								
Student 5																								
Student 6																								
Student 7																								
Student 8																								
Student 9																								
Student 10																								
Student 11																								
Student 12																								
Student 13																								
Student 14																								
Student 15																								
Student 16																								

Supervisor Summary

....

Using curriculum benchmarks to organize the grade book allows teachers and students to clearly understand the reasons behind assigned grades.

○ Remind teachers that grades should reflect benchmark progress.

○ Note that the grid design of green-paper grade books lends itself to organization by benchmarks.

Using Electronic Grade Books

Electronic grade books offer additional possibilities when it comes to analyzing data. When teachers set up an electronic system for scoring by benchmarks, they begin by using a spreadsheet, following the same model shown in Figure 6.1. This allows the clustering of multiple scores per benchmark in order to view performance trends.

It is clear that using an electronic grade book offers advantages, but it requires that teachers and the principal be prepared to make changes. When a principal is willing to introduce and use new technological advances, any initial reluctance teachers have about changing practices may be assuaged, allowing them to feel more supported in making a change. Jennifer, the elementary teacher who saw her green-paper grade book as something very personal, probably also felt a degree of uncertainty about how others would perceive its setup: had she "done it right"? Led by principals who are willing to introduce and use new technology, entire staffs can make the switch to electronic grade books together, allowing them to shape new habits and not feel hindered by past practices.

Peggy Black, coordinator for the Center for Culturally Diverse Learners, reminds us of the story of the ham. During a family gathering, a cook prepares a ham for dinner by cutting off both ends of the meat. One of the younger relatives asks why one would do that. Wasn't it just wasting perfectly good ham? The cook replies, "This is the way we have always done it, from generation to generation." When the youth asks the family matriarch about this longstanding tradition, the explanation is surprising: "Oh, our ovens used to be very small in the old days; if you didn't cut off the ends of the ham, it wouldn't fit into the oven!"

Today's proverbial ovens are larger. We don't need to apologize for our past actions, but we can use technology to track data more efficiently and keep students informed about their progress. In this way, technology and feedback work in conjunction. The idea of criterion-based assessment is not new; remember the mastery learning promises of the behavioral-objective curriculum movement. The instinct to work toward improvement was clear, but the technology was not yet available.

Supervisor Summary

Supervisors who learn to use new technology and support their teachers in doing the same positively affect student learning.
- Explain to teachers that electronic grade books offer advantages of clustering and analyzing data trends in ways that traditional paper grade books do not.
- Collaborate with teachers to use electronic grade books to enrich discussions about data trends and instructional improvement.

Teacher Reports

In addition to making data recording and tracking more efficient, the use of electronic grade books also supports communication between supervisor and teacher about student progress. High school principal Julie Mosher says that using software for grading allows up-to-date access to data and, more important, provides ways to organize and reorganize student performance data in one teacher's classroom as well as across a grade level or subject area.

In Julie's building, Jeff See and other members of the English department began using a grade book program (WebGrader by Collaborative Learning, Inc.) that allows them to score student assignments to benchmarks. Julie observes Jeff's classes, and their post-observation conference activities include using reports generated by WebGrader to analyze student performances.

Jeff described for us three of the reports that have served as catalysts for meaningful discussions with his principal (see Figures 6.2, 6.3, and 6.4). Here, he explains some of the ways they affect the decisions he makes about teaching:

Standards* by Student Report (Figure 6.2)

The "Standards by Student" report is my favorite by far. This report, which can be made available to students and parents on a daily basis, shows an individual student's grades. I enter the grades chronologically as a class activity, and they display by the benchmark. Because I teach English, many of our benchmarks are procedural, and they will appear in multiple assignments or even multiple units. Using this report, I can analyze trends over time by the benchmark.

Many students can now identify three to five benchmarks in the Standards by Student report for which they believe they need improvement. This is a different conversation than "You have four homework assignments to turn in to me if you want a better grade."

Standards Average Report (Figure 6.3)

When my principal and I discuss instructional options, I often bring out the "Standards Average" report. This report displays both calculated average scores and trend proficiency scores for each benchmark assessed. We can evaluate why a class scores particularly low on a benchmark to determine if it is a program, planning, or possibly even a scheduling problem. Even if the average is low, does the trend show students are beginning to improve? I can run this report for all of my classes, and then my principal and I look across the classes for trends. Did one class score higher or lower? If so, do I need to examine individual student performance or reassess the way I deliver instruction in that class? If one class scored above average, what am I doing in that class that I might not be doing in others?

My principal and I may also discuss scores that indicate that *all* classes scored higher or lower on a given benchmark. More important, once all English teachers are scoring to the benchmarks, we will be able make these analyses by department, and comparing our data will have more meaning for program improvement.

*WebGrader uses the term *standards* to mean grade-level curriculum statements.

FIGURE 6.2

WebGrader's Standards by Student Report

English-I   **Student: COOPER, BRENDA**

Teacher: See, Jeff   **Quarter 1 Grade:** 2.55 (B-)
Defined Comments: Late: 0, Incomplete: 0, Excused: 0, Missing: 0   **Report Date:** 10/3/2008

Standard Detail	* - Dropped Late Incomplete Excused Missing			
Standard		Grade	Average	Trend
1 Use reading strategies to understand text				
1.12.1 Use a variety of strategies to extend reading vocabulary			2.75 (B)	3.26 (B+)
Letter from Birmingham - Paper (09/29)		A-		
Writing Assignment 2 (09/17)		B-		
Writing Exercise 1 (09/10)		C		
5 Use the stylistic and rhetorical aspects of writing				
5.12.4 Use a variety of sentence structures and lengths			2.6 (B-)	2.58 (B-)
Letter from Birmingham - Paper (09/29)		B		
Analysis Essay (09/18)		B-		
One-Page Response (09/04)		B-		
Writing Task (08/28)		C		
Paragraph Assignment (08/21)		B		
5.12.5 Use a variety of transitional devices			2.7 (B-)	3.06 (B)
Letter from Birmingham - Paper (09/29)		A-		
Analysis Essay (09/18)		B		
One-Page Response (09/04)		B-		
Writing Task (08/28)		C		
Paragraph Assignment (08/21)		B-		

Class: English-I
Student: COOPER, BRENDA
Topic: 5.12.5 Use a variety of transitional devices

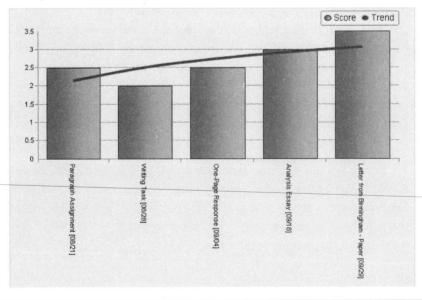

Source: Reprinted courtesy of Brian Sprinkman, WebGrader founder (bsprinkman@pbs-11c.com), and Kevin Baird, Collaborative Learning, Inc.

FIGURE 6.3

WebGrader's Standards Average Report

English-I			See, Jeff

Report Date:	10/3/2008	**Quarter 1 Grade:** 2.66 (B-)

Defined Comments: Late: 0, Incomplete: 0, Excused: 0, Missing: 0

Standard Detail

Standard	Average	Trend Average
1.12.1 Use a variety of strategies to extend reading vocabulary	2.77 (B)	3.3 (A-)
5.12.4 Use a variety of sentence structures and lengths	2.73 (B)	3.05 (B)
5.12.5 Use a variety of transitional devices	2.72 (B)	3.13(B+)

Source: Reprinted courtesy of Brian Sprinkman, WebGrader founder (bsprinkman@pbs-11c.com), and Kevin Baird, Collaborative Learning, Inc.

Standards Not Assessed Report (Figure 6.4)

This may seem obvious, but using the "Standards Not Assessed" report allows me to plan my instruction based on benchmarks I have yet to teach and assess. This report helps me identify which benchmarks need to find their way into my lessons over time. By producing the report to date, I can keep track of how the class performs according to the pacing, and I can seek advice from my principal if I need to do so.

Once he began to score to benchmarks, Jeff spoke with Julie about curriculum concerns. Based on the student data that he had gathered, he realized that the curriculum documents needed some revision. Kathy Golem, the school's curriculum specialist, tells us that teachers now look for their curriculum documents to be continually revised. The days of the "finished" documents sitting on the shelves for years and years is over.

Supervisor Summary

Examining data generated by an electronic grade book is a way to enrich your discussions with teachers to further student progress.

- Analyze individual student achievement trends over time by curriculum benchmarks.
- Examine individual score averages.
- Help teachers plan for instruction for benchmarks that still need to be taught and assessed.

FIGURE 6.4

WebGrader's Standards Not Assessed Report

English-I   **Jeff See**

Report Date: 10/1/2008   **Grade period:** Quarter 1

ENGLISH BENCHMARKS
1 Use reading strategies to understand text
　1.12.2 Understand specific devices that convey meaning
　1.12.3 Use strategies to extend comprehension
2 Critically analyze text
　2.12.1 Analyze author technique in the context of history and culture
　2.12.2 Understand how universal themes are developed in literature
　2.12.3 Understand how literary elements combine to produce a dominant tone, effect or theme
3 Read to acquire information
　3.12.3 Understand and follow written directions
4 Use the general skills and strategies of the writing process
　4.12.1 Use a variety of prewriting strategies
5 Use the stylistic and rhetorical aspects of writing
　5.12.3 Use paragraph form in writing
　5.12.6 Use a variety of techniques to convey a personal style and voice
6 Use grammatical and mechanical conventions
　6.12.1 Use conventions of Standard English in written compositions
　6.12.3 Use conventions of capitalization in written compositions
　6.12.4 Use conventions of punctuation in written compositions
　6.12.7 Use correct agreement
7 Gather and use information for research purposes
　7.12.4 Synthesize information from multiple research studies to draw conclusions
　7.12.6 Present findings in a written format

Source: Reprinted courtesy of Brian Sprinkman, WebGrader founder (bsprinkman@pbs-11c.com), and Kevin Baird, Collaborative Learning, Inc.

Administrator Reports

Brian Sprinkman, the creator of WebGrader, first designed the electronic grade book for teachers but came to realize how useful reports on Standards by Student and Standards Averages could be for supervisors. He went on to design additional reports specifically for supervisors' use. Among many options are the teacher, student, and threshold reports seen Figures 6.5, 6.6, and 6.7.

Teacher Report (Figure 6.5)

This report allows you to look into the class of a specific teacher. Many times administrators are the ones who field calls from parents wondering about a specific grade. This report shows all the work for a class by category and gives the administrator using the system a quick snapshot of the work that has been entered in the class's grade book.

FIGURE 6.5

WebGrader's Teacher Report

Social Studies-3 **Gonzalez, Maria**

Report Date: 10/22/2008 **Quarter 1 Class Average:** 3.5 (B+)
Defined Comments: Late: 0, Incomplete: 0, Excused: 0, Missing: 0

Assignment Information

Key	Category	Assignment	Standards	Due Date	Weight(%)	Max Pts	Average
	Practice Work				**20.00**		**3.31 (B+)**
1		Pre-Assessment	X	[08/29]		30	84.12 (B-)
2		Life on the Prairie		[09/12]		100	86.41 (B)
3		Hills and Valleys		[09/16]		4	2.74 (C+)
4		Prairie Assessment		[09/16]		4	3.03 (B)
5		Cities and Towns		[09/17]		4	3.13 (B)
7		Journeys		[09/17]		4	2.96 (C+)
8		Map Reading Practice	X	[09/19]		75	97.06 (A+)
9		Tales from Town and Country		[09/24]		2	67.65 (D+)
10		Map Skills 1		[10/08]		25	84.47 (B-)
13		Cities - Intro		[10/20]		N/A	N/A
14		Map Reading		[10/20]		25	90.35 (A-)
	Tests and Projects				**80.00**		**3.55 (A)**
6		Early Settlers	X	[09/17]		4	3.29 (B)
11		Map Skills 2		[10/15]		100	89.62 (B+)
12		Map Reading 2	X	[10/17]		50	87.29 (B+)
15		People of the Valley	X	[10/21]		100	92.29 (A-)

Social Studies-3
Student Summary * -

Dropped Late Incomplete Excused Missing

Name	1	2	3	4	5	6	7	8	9	10	11	12	13	14	15						Average
(Max Pts)	30	100	4	4	4	4	4	75		25	100	50		25	100						
Carrillo, Kalin	26	86	2.5	3	3	3.25	3	74	1	22	91	44	√	23	91						3.54 (A)
Carter, David	24	86	2.5	3	3	3.25	3.25	71	1.5	21	89	45	√	21	92						3.53 (A)
Franklin, Jennifer	26	86	2.5	3	3	3.25	3	78	1	21	90	42		23	91						3.42 (B+)
Freeman, Jessica	27	88	2.5	3	3	3.25	3	79	1.25	20	92	44	√	23	91						3.54 (A)
Garza, Trent	28	85	2.5	3	3	3.25	3	73	1.25	21	89	43	√	23	94						3.52 (A)
Hunter, Willie	26	84	2.5	3	3	3	3	73	1	20	89	44		22	91						3.35 (B+)
Jackson, Corey	24	91	3	3.5	3.5	3.5	3.25	71	1.75	18	95	45.5	√	22	95						3.79 (A)
Johnson, Jayda	21	90	2.5	3	3	3.25	3.5	72.5	1.5	22	86	43.5	√	24	96						3.53 (A)
Johnson, Michael	26	89	3	3	3.5	3.25	3	70	1.5	23	87	31	√	23	91						3.2 (B)
Jordan, Trent	29	89	2.5	3		3.25	2.75	69	1.25	21	89	42		25	94						3.54 (A)
Morales, Kevia	30	87	3	3	3.75	3.25	2.5	67	1	19	90	46	√	24	94						3.54 (A)
Rice, Jared	30	83	2.5	3	3.25	3.5	2.25	73.5	1.25	18	91	46	√	23	91						3.56 (A)
Rolf, Deonte	25	82	3	3	3	3.25	2.5	71	1	24	89	44	√	23	93						3.52 (A)
Rosik, Mitchell	23	88	3	3	3	3.25	3	71.5	1.25	23	92.5	47	√	21	91						3.53 (A)
Settles, Adriana	21	81	2.5	3	3.25	3.75	3.25	72	1.5	23	89	44	√	20	92						3.58 (A)
Sharp, Trent	22	85	3	3	3	3.25	3	78	2	22	88	45	√	23	91						3.43 (B+)
Stevenson, Erika	21	89	3.5	3	3	3.25	3	74	2	21	87	46	√	21	91						3.42 (B+)

Source: Reprinted courtesy of Brian Sprinkman, WebGrader founder (bsprinkman@pbs-11c.com), and Kevin Baird, Collaborative Learning, Inc.

Student Report (Figure 6.6)

In the event that an administrator wants to examine a single student's grades, the Student Report provides a detailed look. With this report, the product's usefulness expands beyond administration to apply to coaches, counselors, and other school personnel.

FIGURE 6.6

WebGrader's Student Report

Social Studies-3   **Student: Jackson, Corey**

Teacher: Gonzalez, Maria   **Quarter 1 Grade:** 3.09 (B)
Defined Comments: Late: 0, Incomplete: 0, Excused: 0, Missing: 0   **Report Date:** 10/22/2008

Practice Work - 20%

Name	Due	Pts.	Max Pts.	Grade	% or Rubric	Defined Comments	Unique Comment
Pre-Assessment	[08/29]	24	30	B-	80		Please re-do practice exercises
Life on the Prairie	[09/12]	91	100	A-	91		
Hills and Valleys	[09/16]	3		C+	3		
Prairie Assessment	[09/16]	3.5		B+	3.5		
Cities and Towns	[09/17]	3.5		B+	3.5		
Journeys	[09/17]	3.25		B	3.25		
Map Reading Practice	[09/19]	71	75	A	94.67		
Tales from Town and Country	[09/24]	1.75	2	B+	87.5		
Book Choice 1	[09/26]	89	100	B+	89		
Map Skills 1	[10/08]	18	25	C-	72		This assignment is a Pre-assessment and will be used to show improvement.
Cities - Intro	[10/20]			√			
Map Reading	[10/20]	22	25	B+	88		
Totals				**B+**	**3.43**		

Tests and Projects - 80%

Name	Due	Pts.	Max Pts.	Grade	% or Rubric	Defined Comments	Unique Comment
Map Project	[09/02]	321	400	D-	80.25		Please review mapping - see p. 10
History Project	[09/10]	2.5		C	2.5		
Early Settlers	[09/17]	3.5		B+	3.5		
Glaciers	[09/18]	44	50	B+	88		
Book Choice 2	[09/26]	94	100	A	94		
Map Skills 2	[10/15]	95	100	A	95		
Map Reading 2	[10/17]	45.5	50	A-	91		
People of the Valley	[10/21]	95	100	A	95		
Totals				**C+**	**3**		

Source: Reprinted courtesy of Brian Sprinkman, WebGrader founder (bsprinkman@pbs-11c.com), and Kevin Baird, Collaborative Learning, Inc.

Threshold Report (Figure 6.7)

The concept behind the Threshold Report was to allow the administrator the ability to determine which students at this grade level and subject area are struggling, and on which benchmarks. In this screenshot, WebGrader identified all 3rd grade students who received a proficiency rating of "1" on their report cards.

It is possible that the particular benchmark was newly introduced and that a higher proficiency rating was not expected at that time. Therefore, the report can link to another that shows how well the entire class performed on that particular benchmark. This gives the administrator a way to see how the class performs on this particular benchmark. If a student needs to improve on a benchmark, the student's name links to the Standards by Student report, to gauge how he or she is doing on the rest of the benchmarks.

FIGURE 6.7
WebGrader's Threshold Report

Threshold Report - Standards Analysis

Report Criteria

Data Used:	Report Card	**Length:**	Quarter 1
Grade Level:	3	**Proficiency Key(s):**	1

Students Meeting Threshold Criteria

Student	Subject	Teacher	Topic	Grade
Johnson, Jayda	Social Studies	Gonzalez, Maria	Demonstrates knowledge of concepts related to people and events throughout history	1
Johnson, Jayda	Social Studies	Gonzalez, Maria	Demonstrates knowledge of concepts related to the purpose of laws and government	1
Rice, Jared	Mathematics	Fiorenza, Anna	Knows multiplication facts (0-5)	1
Rice, Jared	Mathematics	Fiorenza, Anna	Understands and uses geometric language (two-dimensional, three-dimensional, and symmetry)	1
Rice, Jared	Mathematics	Fiorenza, Anna	Understands place value (whole numbers up to 5 digits)	1
Rosik, Mitchell	Science	Gonzalez, Maria	Earth and Space Science	1

Source: Reprinted courtesy of Brian Sprinkman, WebGrader founder (bsprinkman@pbs-11c.com), and Kevin Baird, Collaborative Learning, Inc.

Recording Versus Reporting

Like many other electronic grade book programs, such as PowerSchool or Infinite Campus, WebGrader can process the teacher's class data into a report card; therefore, it is useful to clarify what we mean by recording versus reporting. The audience for the records in a grade book is primarily the teacher and the student; using an electronic grade book to track scores by benchmarks over a quarter or semester allows the teacher and student to discuss trends in performance. Reporting implies developing a report card, for which the audience is generally parents or guardians. The way to improve student learning is to train teachers to give students feedback in the class, document scores by benchmarks, and regularly display scores to learners in reports such as the Standards by Student report to show the trends. It is a courtesy to parents and guardians to use the software to generate either a traditional report card or a standards report. Parents or guardians who want to see more detail, such as the benchmark-level reports or activities by other categories, can view them just as the teacher and student view the Standards by Student report, either in a printed version or online.

Too often, we see principals decide to become "standards based" by creating a report card committee, believing that if they change the report card, grading practices will change. But changing a report card doesn't change grading practices, and it doesn't improve learning. Changing scoring or record-keeping practices to include benchmark-based scoring *does* improve learning, even if the report card continues to take a traditional form.

Supervisor Summary

Electronic grade books support efforts to tailor student performance data for different audiences.

- Prompt teachers to use records of feedback related to student progress to motivate students and inform teaching decisions.
- Suggest teachers send home records of individual student progress on benchmarks to keep parents and guardians informed.
- Release reports of group progress on curriculum benchmarks or standards to the general public, district offices, and state departments.

Homework, Tests, and Common Assessments

We chose to leave homework and testing for the end of the book because we wanted to emphasize using the Teaching Schema for Master Learners to guide classroom instruction and learning for both the teacher and the students, with emphasis on formative feedback. Because homework tends to be a controversial issue, the prudent suggestion for a principal to make is that teachers clearly tie homework to the benchmarks and give students feedback on it in a timely way but use trend scoring to capitalize on the "practice" nature. Using trend scoring helps ensure the homework is both practice and part of student growth; it should not become a tug-of-war for points. If teachers begin to view homework scores as problematic, the principal will usually be able to identify a likely "instructional problem" to address through supervision.

Administering tests and creating common assessments are critical for summative assessment and program review. Principals should help teachers carefully align these tasks with the benchmarks and track the resulting data appropriately. Of course, these scores are part of each teacher's grade book.

Making the Gains

Do you remember Edward Rooney, the school administrator from the movie *Ferris Bueller's Day Off?* In the film, popular 17-year-old Ferris Bueller and two friends skip school for a day to explore Chicago. The movie chronicles their adventures and Mr. Rooney's desperate, parallel quest to catch the truants. Meanwhile, back at school, the economics teacher pleads for class participation, repeatedly asking the infamous question, "Anyone? Anyone?" The English teacher lectures tediously while students paint their fingernails, read comics, and gaze mindlessly out of the window. It's not a leap to conclude Mr. Rooney's school would be lot a better off if he spent his days supervising teachers and helping them improve their students' learning instead of chasing after Ferris.

Working with teachers to organize planning, instructional delivery, and data collection in ways that ensure learning success requires that principals set priorities in their jobs in order to focus on student achievement. But it only works if the supervisor is able to devote attention to them and does not get distracted by other job demands. Every instructional leader has the "Ferris

Buellers" that nibble away at his or her time: the traffic knot in the designated drop-off area, the schedule interruptions, the new construction project, impromptu but important meetings. Sharon and her colleagues noted that sometimes in the "busy-ness" of situations, we neglect to provide systematic feedback about individual or team performance (Martin et al., 1997).

Every decade ushers in a new set of Ferris Buellers, in the form of both students and school reforms. The goal and challenge for each principal is to set student safety and learning as priorities. This may mean rethinking and reprioritizing the daily tasks, some of which may need to be delegated in order to allow the principal time to support teachers and students.

Sharon recalls that when prospective students interviewed for admittance into the graduate program in the School of Education at the University of Colorado at Denver to pursue a principal's license, she and her faculty colleagues always questioned them about their reasons for wanting to become a principal. Nearly all applicants stated that they wanted to have a broader effect on student learning than they did with just the students in their own classes. Yet after they completed their training and entered into administrative jobs, they frequently found themselves facing "administrivia," rather than achieving their goal of increasing student learning.

To positively affect learners beyond one classroom, principals such as Layne Parmenter work with teachers to apply new strategies and research available to improve learning through supervision. Recently, he sent us this e-mail:

> I was in the process of scheduling with Rita to watch a lesson, and she said, "It doesn't matter when you come; I GANAG all my lessons now." "GANAG" is just part of our school vocabulary now. Coach Roberts came in today and said, "When do you want to come and GANAG?" In 3rd grade, Gordon continues to "GANAC" (because he likes the word "closure"), which is fine with me.
>
> I have a much better perspective now as I'm evaluating teachers about the quality of their lessons and teaching. I completed a final evaluation today, and I could write about the teacher's growth over the past year. I confidently talk with teachers now, and I know I've given teachers more feedback than I ever did before. It never ceases to amaze me: I learn something new about GANAG every single time I watch a lesson.

Mike, the teacher we met in the Introduction, has not only transformed student results but also changed how he works with his principal. Here's a recent update from him:

> It's been a while since we talked, but every time I calculate my grades at the semester, I feel the need to check in with you. I switched over to using electronic standards-based grading on Easy Grade Pro almost exclusively now. In my transition first semester, I continued to track percentages as well as rubric scores for benchmarks. I use the more recent demonstrations rather than the earlier ones because English is so procedural. At the end of first term, I had six students failing. Now at the semester break, only one ended up with a failing grade. (Remember, I used to give Ds or Fs to more than 25 percent of my students.) But we have a semester to go; I think I can get to him.
>
> On another note, my principal is excited about the work, and I enjoy our relationship more now that I can talk about grades. I had the chance to teach a couple of building-level and district staff development classes about criterion-based grading, specifically using electronic recordkeeping. As a result, a math teacher is moving to rubric-scored objectives; we laugh because math teachers tell me they don't change easily. The department chair has asked me to teach more classes this summer, when teachers have time to begin to look at their curricula and really try to implement the change. One teacher at a time, eh? Hey, that would be a good title for a book!

The belief we share as educators in the United States—*that all children will have equal opportunity to learn*—guides our practices away from inspection and toward helping teachers help learners get better. School supervisors play a major role in this improvement.

Supervisor Voice

Linda Law, Curriculum Director

Linda Law, director of secondary curriculum in a New York school district, transformed her communications with the teachers she observed when she started using the Teaching Schema for Master Learners. The shift from "watching the teachers teach" to collaborating about learning has made supervision an entirely more appealing process.

Curriculum's Common Ground

Benjamin Bloom was right. He recommended "that curriculums should facilitate the exchange of information about curricular developments and evaluation devices," but he also warned that "too frequently what appears to be common ground disappears on closer examination of the descriptive terms being used" (1956, p. 1). As a director of curriculum and instruction, I supervise and evaluate teachers on a daily basis and always refer to curriculum documents when I talk with these teachers about their instructional practices. I have found that few teachers know how to use curriculum documents to guide their daily classroom lessons. Some even insert terms from other documents to serve as their lesson objectives, making it impossible to score students to curriculum benchmarks and leading both the teacher and me to revise lesson plans in order to work on "common ground" in our discussions.

When I began my job as curriculum director, our district had just started to revise its curriculum documents using the Big Four tenets (Pollock, 2007). This was a beginning of establishing "common ground" for our work. I found the second step of the Big Four, the Teaching Schema for Master Learners, to be particularly valuable in my work supervising teachers; in fact, the Schema inspired me to make changes to my own practices—changes that I am still making, even as I write this. In my supervisory training, we were taught primarily to observe teachers for evaluation rather than for the purpose of improving student learning. I've found that implementing the Schema gives me the guidance I needed to do this. Specifically, I have altered two aspects of my supervision techniques: (1) how I interact with teachers and help them learn to score students using curriculum targets, and (2) how I help teachers modify lessons so thinking skills, rather than just activity completion, are explicitly required.

Supervising Teachers, but to What End?

When I began evaluating teachers more than 10 years ago, I perceived my role as being the instructional leader for the building. I learned clinical supervision steps, but because the pre-observation conference was negotiable (depending on tenure status of the teacher) and because I was so busy, I conducted these conferences only rarely. During the observation itself, I focused on teacher behaviors. And the post-observation conference consisted of me asking the teacher to reflect back on the lesson and the two of us discussing topics based on the teacher's perceptions. These were great conversations, but looking back, I realize that my suggestions often mirrored those identified by the teacher; for example, we may have come to the conclusion that small-group instruction was a better strategy for a certain concept than whole-class tasks. My written observations recounted the activities I saw unfold in the lesson, but I didn't structure them in a way that would make them useful feedback for the teacher.

Although I had a checklist of topics to discuss, I humbly "fess up" to my personal objectives for observations: to catch the teacher demonstrating a behavior I could compliment during the post-observation conference. I wanted to confirm that the teacher was doing his or her job as a "good" teacher; such compliments would help maintain a positive school culture (or so we were taught in our graduate classes). After all, our goal as supervisors was to improve teaching, assuming it would improve learning. What better way to improve teachers' performance than by praising them for a job well done? My comments were always sincere, and I believe that both the teachers and I left the meeting feeling that we had made a positive connection. But when I learned about the Big Four and the Teaching Schema for Master Learners, I realized I needed to change my supervision if I wanted to *really* help teachers improve student achievement.

Essential Guidance for Curriculum and Instruction

The Schema provides valuable guidance for my supervisory work with teachers, and in conversations with them about their teaching practices, I often share the following key tenets:

1. Really use a curriculum document, rather than just cutting and pasting standards on old lessons to make them look legitimate. If the curriculum documents are not right for your purposes, revise them.

2. Assiduously match your instructional strategy to the goal of the lesson (curriculum benchmark and objectives). The time students spend working on the task you have planned for them should advance their skills and understanding.

3. Continually match the evaluation of student progress with the lesson's goal or benchmark. Track the data in a systematic way to see whether or not you, as a teacher, can modify, re-teach, or differentiate instruction to help learners learn before they move on to another grade or course.

In my supervision of nontenured teachers, I always include a pre-observation conference, in part because it provides a great opportunity for me to share these three tenets. The pre-observation conference, or what we fondly call the "pre-flection," has become nonnegotiable and is structured using the Schema to ensure a focus on improving student learning. I've learned that if I'm going to affect instruction, I can have as great an impact before the lesson as I can after the fact—perhaps more. Instead of waiting for the post-observation conference to speak about corrective feedback, I guide the teacher in making changes before the lesson takes place. The discussion about learning in the pre-observation conference sets the criteria for the observation.

Also, during the pre-observation conference, I remind the teacher to reflect on the curricular goal as it relates to each activity. The importance of this comes to light when I physically fold over the lesson plan so that the goal and assessment are next to each other and ask the teacher if they match. What this usually exposes is that the teacher views assessment as it pertains to the activity rather than to the curriculum benchmarks, so I recommend a shift in viewpoint.

Often, rather than using curriculum documents to develop lesson objectives, teachers design lessons and then "attach" state standards as objectives; this is the kind of a cut-and-paste process that is a detriment to "common ground." These standards are by no means specific enough to drive a lesson in which the teacher could give feedback to learners to help them improve.

During one pre-observation conference, an English teacher provided me with a lesson plan that used the Hunter format and identified broad state standards as its objectives. She was unable to state how feedback to learners would specifically relate to curriculum benchmarks. In another example, the teacher had identified the state standards and a reasonable set of more specific benchmarks. She then converted the standards and benchmarks into questions. This information took up a page of the observation form. When I asked which statements she would use to give criterion-based feedback to her students, she wasn't sure.

Not only is it important that lesson goals be developed from curriculum benchmarks, but it is important, also, that activities relating to these goals stimulate higher-level thinking in students. An example of one of my observations of class activities that fell short of this goal occurred with a social studies teacher whose lesson focused on how militarism, imperialism, nationalism, and totalitarianism contributed to the outbreak of World War II. Because the lesson revolved around declarative knowledge, the teacher appropriately used a PowerPoint presentation and an accompanying organizer for students to take notes. At the end of class, students left an exit ticket that the teacher used to assess their understanding of the four main causes of the war. The assessment of students' knowledge of details was fair. They did apply lower-level knowledge-gathering skills, but they were not asked to demonstrate higher-order processing skills to use this knowledge in problem solving or decision making. Even though there was time for students to work together in compiling and sharing their notes, they were not required to think—they did not discuss, argue, or try to draw conclusions from messy content. This class was a clear example of the distinction in the Schema between gathering information and using thinking skills.

We are now beginning to work districtwide on changing our scoring and record keeping to generate much better information. Although it has been difficult for some teachers to make the changes, they tell me the effort required is worth it, because the data they now have is helping them improve their instruction.

I am realizing the importance of the supervisor in (1) helping teachers write lesson objectives developed from curriculum documents, (2) ensuring that they consistently give criterion-based feedback to students, and (3) working with them to develop challenging class activities that require students to use higher-level thinking skills. Through my supervision, I work one-on-one with teachers to discuss the new research on feedback and actually help them make changes to their practices. We talk, I watch, and then we get to talk again to find out what changes worked best. Every teacher is grateful for the feedback. In the past, no one would try to find me after an observation just to continue the discussion. Now I'm feeling downright popular! In fact, teachers actually invite me back to observe them after their observation requirement has been met.

The Schema Is Contagious

During the past three years, I've learned to change my supervision one principal at a time by working with one teacher at a time. Instead of mandating that all teachers use the Teaching Schema for Master Learners or score to benchmarks, our district has taken an indirect but systematic approach to their promotion. As teachers have started to use Schema strategies, they have informally mentored others, and the work has spread organically. Our district is seeing gains in both student communication and student achievement.

As a supervisor, I have learned lessons of my own. I now realize that time spent on a pre-observation conference is priceless and that both novice and veteran teachers value useful corrective feedback—not just praise. As educators, we thrive on "getting better," and we *know* that we are getting better when our students show us that they, too, are getting better, thanks to our decision to structure lessons in a way that gives them optimal feedback.

Afterword:
The Incentive to Teach and
Supervise Teaching

THE IDEAS WE PUT FORTH IN THIS BOOK BRING US, JANE AND SHARON, FULL CIRCLE. In the mid-1980s, each of us independently conducted research for our doctoral dissertations to determine levels of job satisfaction for elementary and secondary teachers in Colorado relative to their expectations about working in the profession. We did this research under the supervision of Michael Martin, then a professor at the University of Colorado and project coordinator for a statewide educational reform initiative, the 2 + 2 Project, directed by Irv Moskowitz. Two major goals of this comprehensive project were to identify characteristics of good teachers and principals and to identify incentives to retain them. Our research contributed to the project goals.

Two job characteristics that we examined in our earlier research, *job advancement* and *recognition*, were areas in which teachers did not feel that their expectations met the realities of their on-the-job work. Twenty years ago, the most common advancement opportunity for teachers was to move into the ranks of administration. Today, there are additional avenues for teachers' career advancement, including becoming mentors, master teachers, peer coaches, and building resource teachers. Of course, many excellent teachers still move into positions as principals, often citing a desire to have a more widespread effect on student achievement through work with teachers as a reason for doing so. To us, the implications are clear: the strongest hope of educators, what they are most passionate about, is the opportunity to positively influence student learning and success.

It is human nature to desire recognition. Teachers work with great passion, and yet success for their students is often influenced by complicated social factors. Principals want to recognize their teachers and to help them plan for the everyday successes that are the foundation for major gains in student achievement. But even principals who were excellent teachers themselves can struggle to articulate for their staff the teaching methods they used so effectively when they were in the classroom. In Chapter 1, we pondered the question of why some supervisory visits to classrooms are viewed as supportive while others are dreaded and seen as occasional events of perfunctory judgment. After reading this book, we hope you will agree with us that the question can be answered by considering the degree to which principals and supervisors—those who have advanced in and beyond teaching—can remain in touch with teaching and learning in ways that effectively recognize important components of student learning, and then go on to assist teachers in incorporating these components into their planning and teaching. The Teaching Schema for Master Learners offers the steps necessary to do this. Using the Schema, principals can provide the meaningful recognition their teachers want and deserve, and they can receive the positive recognition from teachers that they want: to be seen as supporters rather than as evaluators doling out judgment.

Let's review the ways in which the Teaching Schema for Master Learners incorporates essential goals for improvement. When we work toward school improvement, we act to improve three things:

1. *Student learning.* Research shows that all learners can learn to think and construct new ideas or processes.

2. *Pedagogical automaticity.* Research shows that teachers affect student learning every day.

3. *Communication.* We know leadership is the key to foster staffwide ownership of the previous two goals—and this ownership is essential for improvement.

It is clear to us that the Teaching Schema for Master Learners can boost not only student learning, pedagogical automacity, and communication, but job satisfaction for both teachers and supervisors. It offers conditions for increased and positive recognition of teachers by supervisors and of supervisors by teachers. In this way, it addresses what the field of supervision has struggled for more than a century to achieve: being a means of improving learning rather than inspecting teaching.

Teachers tell us that they stay in the profession because they believe they positively affect student learning every day. In fact, improved student learning as a direct result of good teaching may be the teacher's primary incentive to stay on the job. Teachers become good or great teachers using methods such as the Teaching Schema for Master Learners—ones that structure learning around how a learner learns best rather than just how a teacher teaches best. And teachers benefit from the guidance of and feedback from supervisors who respond to the same incentive: improved learning for *all* students.

Acknowledgments

Our thanks to the following individuals:

Susan Alexander, Amy Ashton, Jen Au Claire, Sara Austin, Rob Becker, Peggy Black, Jackie Campbell, Tony Cardamone, Janna Cochrane, Monique Conway, Kirk Delwiche, Norberto Diaz, Paul Dix, Jeff Farrington, Gail Goff, Kathy Golem, Julie Goodelle, Francine Grannell, Andrew Haney, Dan Hanrahan, Edwina Hay, Amanda Haynes, Barbara Herzog, Brian Holzman, Anne Hughes, Andy Jones, Melissa Julian, Erin Kohl, Jami Kohl, Jon Langstaff, Linda Law, Camille Leisten, Kristie Lyon, Michael Martin, Bruce McMurray, Kathy Mohr, Julie Mosher, Dwight Mott, Scott Norton, Gary Nunnally, Terry Osman, Layne Parmenter, Dana Paykos, David Peabody, Jim Perkins, Sharon Pernisi, Diane Quirk, Gillian Reeves, George Santos, Bess Scott, David Seabast, Jeff See, Brian Sprinkman, Jenny Thomes, Daniel Todd, Bonnie Van Benschoten, Corine Van den Wildenberg, Jennifer Webber, Therese Weiler, Becky White, Dana Zigler, and Richard Zimman.

Our special thanks to Scott Willis, Katie Martin, and the ASCD publications staff for their continuous support and interest in improving student learning.

References and Resources

Acheson, K. A., & Gall, M. D. (1980). *Techniques in the clinical supervision of teachers*. White Plains, NY: Longman.

Aseltine, J. M., Faryniarz, J. O., & Rigazio-DiGilio, A. J. (2006). *Supervision for learning: A performance-based approach to teacher development and school improvement*. Alexandria, VA: Association for Supervision and Curriculum Development.

Bloom, B. (Ed.). (1956). *Taxonomy of educational objectives*. New York: David McKay Company.

Blumberg, A. (1980). *Supervisors and teachers: A private cold war* (2nd ed.). Berkeley, CA: McCutcheon.

Boone, L. E., & Bowen, D. D. (1980). *The great writings in management and organizational behavior*. Tulsa, OK: The Petroleum Publishing Company.

Borg, W. R., & Gall, M. D. (1983). *Educational research: An introduction* (4th ed.). New York: Longman.

Carnegie Forum on Education and the Economy Task Force on Teaching as a Profession. (1986). *A nation prepared: Teachers for the 21st century*. New York: Carnegie Forum on Education.

Christen, W. L., & Murphy, T. J. (1991). *Increasing comprehension by activating prior knowledge*. (Report no. 1991-03-00). Bloomington, IN: ERIC Clearinghouse on Reading and Communication Skills. (ERIC Document Reproduction Service No. ED328885)

Cogan, M. L. (1973). *Clinical supervision*. Boston: Houghton Mifflin.

Conley, D. (2005). *College knowledge: What it really takes for students to succeed and what we can do to get them ready*. San Francisco: Jossey-Bass.

Costa, A., & Garmston, R. (1985, February). Supervision for intelligent teaching. *Educational Leadership, 42*(5), 70–80.

Costa, A., & Garmston, R. (1994). *Cognitive coaching: A foundation for renaissance schools*. Norwood, MA: Christopher-Gordon Publishers, Inc.

Costa, A., & Kallick, B. (2000). *Habits of mind: A developmental series*. Alexandria, VA: Association for Supervision and Curriculum Development.

Cremin, L. A. (Ed.). (1957). *The republic and the school*. New York: Teachers College, Columbia University.

Danielson, C. (2007). *Enhancing professional practice: A framework for teaching* (2nd ed.). Alexandria, VA: Association for Supervision and Curriculum Development.

Doidge, N. (2007). *The brain that changes itself*. New York: Penguin Books.

Downey, C., Steffy, B., English, F., Frase, L., & Poston, W. (2004). *The three-minute classroom walk-through: Changing school supervisory practice one teacher at a time*. Thousand Oaks, CA: Corwin Press.

Eisner, E. W. (1982). An artistic approach to supervision. In T. J. Sergiovanni (Ed.), *Supervision of teaching* (pp. 53–66). Alexandria, VA: Association for Supervision and Curriculum Development.

Finn, C. E., Jr., Julian, L., & Petrelli, M. J. (2006). *State of the state standards.* Washington, DC: Thomas B. Fordham Foundation and Institute. (ERIC Document Reproduction Service No. ED493851) Available: www.edexcellence.net

Ford, S., Muth, R., Martin, M., & Murphy, M. (1996). *Performance assessment: The real world of educational leadership.* Paper presented at the annual meeting of the University Council for Educational Administration, Louisville, KY.

Gawande, A. (2007). *Better: A surgeon's notes on performance.* New York: Metropolitan Books.

Glanz, J. (1991). *Bureaucracy and professionalism: The evolution of public school supervision.* Rutherford, NJ: Farleigh Dickinson University Press.

Glatthorn, A. A. (1984). *Differentiated supervision.* Alexandria, VA: Association for Supervision and Curriculum Development.

Glickman, C. (1985). *Supervision of instruction: A developmental approach.* Boston: Allyn & Bacon.

Goldhammer, R. (1969). *Clinical supervision: Special methods for the supervision of teachers.* New York: Holt, Rinehart, & Winston.

Guskey, T., & Bailey, J. (2001). *Developing grading and reporting systems for student learning.* Thousand Oaks, CA: Corwin Press.

Gutek, G. L. (1991). *Education in the United States: An historical perspective.* Needham Heights, MA: Allyn & Bacon.

Hattie, J., & Timperley, H. (2007). The power of feedback. *Review of Educational Research, 77*(1), 81–112.

Hunter, M. (1980, February). Six types of supervisory conferences. *Educational Leadership, 37*(5), 408–412.

Hunter, M. (1982). *Mastery teaching.* Thousand Oaks, CA: Corwin Press.

International Center for Leadership in Education. (2008). *Rigor and relevance series.* Available: www.leadered.com/rrresources.html

International Society for Technology in Education. (2008). *National educational technology standards for students* (2nd ed.). Washington, DC: Author. Available: www.iste.org

Johnson, D. W., & Johnson, R. T. (1999). *Learning together and alone: Cooperative, competitive, and individualistic learning.* Boston: Allyn & Bacon.

Joyce, B., & Showers, B. (1988). *Student achievement through staff development.* New York: Longman.

Kagan Publishing and Profesional Development [Web site]. Available: www.kaganonline.com

Leeper, R. R. (1969). *Changing supervision for changing times: Addresses for the 24th Annual Conference.* Washington, DC: Association for Supervision and Curriculum Development.

Martin, M., Ford, S., Murphy, M., Rehm, R., & Muth, R. (1997). Linking instructional delivery with diverse learning settings. *Journal of School Leadership, 7*(4), 386–408.

Marzano, R. J. (2000). *Transforming grading.* Alexandria, VA: Association for Supervision and Curriculum Development.

Marzano, R. J., Pickering, D. J., & Pollock, J. E. (2001). *Classroom instruction that works: Research-based strategies for increasing student achievement.* Alexandria, VA: Association for Supervision and Curriculum Development.

McGreal, T. L. (1983). *Successful teacher evaluation.* Alexandria, VA: Association for Supervision and Curriculum Development.

Mosher, R. L., & Purpel, D. E. (1972). *Supervision: The reluctant profession.* New York: Houghton Mifflin.

O'Connor, K. (2002). *How to grade for learning.* Thousand Oaks, CA: Corwin Press.

Ogle, D. S. (1986). K-W-L group instructional strategy. In A. S. Palincsar, D. S. Ogle, B. F. Jones, & E. G. Carr (Eds.), *Teaching reading as thinking* (Teleconference Resource Guide, pp. 11–17). Alexandria, VA: Association for Supervision and Curriculum Development.

Oliva, P. (1989). *Supervision for today's schools*. New York: Longman.

Ornstein, A., & Levine, D. (1993). *Foundations of education* (5th ed.). Boston: Houghton Mifflin.

Pajak, E. (1993). *Approaches to clinical supervision: Alternatives for improving instruction*. Norwood, MA: Christopher-Gordon Publishers, Inc.

Pollock, J. E. (2007). *Improving student learning one teacher at a time*. Alexandria, VA: Association for Supervision and Curriculum Development.

Sergiovanni, T. J., & Starratt, R. J. (1993). *Supervision: A redefinition* (5th ed.). New York: McGraw-Hill.

Sullivan, S., & Glanz, J. (2005). *Supervision that improves teaching*. Thousand Oaks, CA: Corwin Press.

Taylor, F. W. (1916). *The principles of scientific management*. New York: Harper Brothers.

Tucker, P. D., & Stronge, J. H. (2005). *Linking teacher evaluation and student learning*. Alexandria, VA: Association for Supervision and Curriculum Development.

U.S. Department of Education National Commission on Excellence in Education. (1983). *A nation at risk: The imperative for educational reform*. Washington, DC: Author. Available: www.ed.gov/pubs/NatAtRisk/index.html

U.S. Department of Education National Education Goals Panel. (1994). *Goals 2000: Educate America Act*. Washington, DC: Author. Available: www.ed.gov/legislation/GOALS2000/TheAct/index.html

Willis, J. (2006). *Research-based strategies to ignite student learning*. Alexandria, VA: Association for Supervision and Curriculum Development.

Index

Note: The letter *f* following a page number denotes a figure. GANAG steps are shown capitalized.

About the Authors

Jane E. Pollock is the director of Learning Horizon, Inc. Specializing in the areas of teaching and supervising learning, Dr. Pollock consults on long-term contracts with schools worldwide to improve student learning and teaching practices. She is the author of *Improving Student Learning One Teacher at a Time* (2007) and the coauthor of *Dimensions of Learning Teacher and Training Manuals* (1996), *Assessment, Grading and Record Keeping* (1999), and *Classroom Instruction That Works* (2000). She is an adjunct faculty member for the Association for Supervision and Curriculum Development and various universities in the United States. A native of Caracas, Venezuela, Dr. Pollock earned degrees at the University of Colorado and Duke University. She can be reached by e-mail at jepollock@improvestudentlearning.com.

Sharon M. Ford most recently served as an assistant professor in the graduate department of Administrative Leadership and Policy Studies in the School of Education and Human Development at the University of Colorado at Denver, where the primary focus of her work was the field of supervision. She advised numerous doctoral and master's degree students and taught courses for graduate students seeking licenses as school principals and superintendents. Prior to that post, Dr. Ford worked for a state department of education, served in an administrative role in a large school district, and taught in regular and special education classrooms. Dr. Ford's work has appeared in many refereed journals, including the *Journal of School Leadership, The Executive Educator,*

Educational Administration Quarterly, and a National Council of Professors of Educational Administration yearbook. She served as the regional representative for a seven-state area to the Professors of Secondary School Administration, National Association of Secondary School Principals, and was president of the Colorado Association of Professors of School Administration. Dr. Ford earned degrees at the University of Colorado and Whittier College. She can be reached at sharonf3@earthlink.net.

Related ASCD Products

For the most up-to-date information about ASCD resources, go to www.ascd.org. ASCD stock numbers are noted in parentheses.

Books

Building Teachers' Capacity for Success: A Collaborative Approach for Coaches and School Leaders by Pete Hall and Alisa Simeral (#109002)

The Handbook for Enhancing Professional Practice: Using the Framework for Teaching in Your School by Charlotte Danielson (#106035)

How to Help Your School Thrive Without Breaking the Bank by John Gabriel and Paul Farmer (#107042)

Improving Student Learning One Teacher at a Time by Jane E. Pollock (#107005)

Learning and Leading with Habits of Mind: 16 Essential Characteristics for Success edited by Arthur L. Costa and Bena Kallick (#108008)

Qualities of Effective Principals by James H. Stronge, Holly B. Richard and Nancy Catano (#108003)

Downloads

Electronic Forms and Rubrics for Enhancing Professional Practice: A Framework for Teaching by Charlotte Danielson (#108123DL)

Teacher Evaluation & Teacher Portfolios: An ASCD Electronic Topic Pack (#197202E)

Video

The How To Collection: Instruction That Promotes Learning (six 15-minute video programs on one 110-minute DVD) (#606141)

A Visit to Classrooms of Effective Teachers (one 45-minute program with a comprehensive Viewer's Guide) (DVD: #605026, videotape: #405026)

THE WHOLE CHILD The Whole Child Initiative helps schools and communities create learning environments that allow students to be healthy, safe, engaged, supported, and challenged. To learn more about other books and resources that relate to the whole child, visit www.wholechildeducation.org.

For more information, visit us on the World Wide Web (http://www.ascd.org), send an e-mail message to member@ascd.org, call the ASCD Service Center (1-800-933-ASCD or 703-578-9600, then press 2), send a fax to 703-575-5400, or write to Information Services, ASCD, 1703 N. Beauregard St., Alexandria, VA 22311-1714 USA.